CONTENTS

Introduction 4

Cats 8

Dogs 28

Small Mammals

    Rabbits 52

    Houserabbits 61

    Guinea pigs 66

    Rats 74

    Mice 82

    Hamsters 90

    Gerbils 106

    Chinchillas 112

    Ferrets 120

Fish 128

Birds 162

Photographic gallery 97

Lancaster & Morecambe College
The Hexagon

T36875

Animal Care - 636.0887

Donation | 30/9/13

COMPLETE PETS HANDBOOK

igloo

Published by Igloo Books Limited
Henson Way
Telford Way Industrial Estate
Kettering
Northants
NN16 8PX
info@igloo-books.com

This edition published 2005

All rights reserved. No part of this publication may be reproduced, stored in a retrieval system, or transmitted, in any form or by any means, electronic, mechanical, photocopying, recording or otherwise, without written permission in accordance with the provisions of the Copyright Act 1956 (as amended). Any person or persons who do any unauthorised act in relation to this publication may be liable to criminal prosecution and civil claim for damages.

© Copyright Igloo Books Ltd

ISBN 1-84561-080-6

Project management Kandour

Printed in India

Introduction

PET

noun 1 a domestic or tamed animal or bird kept for companionship or pleasure. 2 a person treated with special favour. 3 used as an affectionate form of address.

This pretty much sums up the regard in which we human beings hold the domesticated animals that share our lives. We sometimes go as far as relating to them as small people, and we certainly address them with affection, so, in essence, every definition of the noun 'pet' applies.

But why do we keep pets? What gave our ancestors the idea to keep animals as pets? Well, the answer is, initially, they were kept for practical reasons. Our cave-dwelling ancestors happened upon the idea of domesticating wolves. Most likely, a litter of wolf cubs were captured and confined with a view to being eaten. Maybe someone saw that these young animals could display emotion towards human beings – fear, certainly, but maybe also deference, seeing the humans as superior wolves, higher members of the pack. In this way, the wolf pups were maybe not eaten, but instead tamed, nurtured, allowed to mature and, crucially, taught to hunt alongside human hunters and work for humans. Not only could they hunt, they could guard the cave against intruders, such as bears, lions, other wolves and human interlopers. Thus, out of practicality, the dog was developed.

Cats too were domesticated and evolved in much the same way, used mainly for hunting vermin and thus preserving crops and grain stores. Other animals were domesticated as the

INTRODUCTION

centuries passed – cows, pigs, poultry, horses, rabbits, and cavies. Many of these were far more practical in nature, while dogs, cats, rabbits and cavies began to be seen more as companions than working tools. As life for human beings became less a matter of day-to-day survival, animals could be indulged, they wouldn't necessarily need to work. They would fill a need in our lives for beauty, companionship and affection.

Now, thousands of years on from those first wolf pups tamed by ancient humans, most households have a pet of some description, often more than one. In fact, pets are very much a part of our daily lives.

Pets are good for us

Pets are good for our health – and that's official.

A health psychologist and senior research fellow at a leading British university undertook extensive research which found that exposure to cats and/or dogs in the first year of life reduced subsequent risks of allergic sensitisation during childhood and that exposure to pets is associated with a significantly reduced risk of asthma.

This research also provided an insight into how children and pets interact. A survey of 338 children found that:

40% sought out their pet if they were upset
40% looked for their pet if they were bored
85% regard their pets as a playmate
53% watched TV or videos with their pet

There have been numerous scientific studies undertaken to show that adults as well as children benefit physically and mentally from pet ownership. Simply owning a dog can prompt people to take regular exercise by walking the dog each day, while the need to look after a pet animal gives people – especially older people – an incentive, which keeps them mentally agile.

INTRODUCTION

Keeping pets has been shown to reduce stress levels. Did you know that simply watching a tank of fish swimming to and fro lowers the heart rate and promotes a sense of well-being? Affection displayed by even the smallest of pets to their owners can prompt all sorts of positive bodily and mental reactions in human beings. Pets can even help us to recover more quickly from illnesses.

Keeping a pet

The chances are that you want to keep a pet of your own, or, if you are a parent, that your child wants a pet. There are plenty of factors to consider before you take that step, including:

- the age of the child
- the amount of space available for the animal
- what the pet is going to cost in both money and time
- whether you and your child actually want a pet!

Anybody who is considering getting a pet for themselves or their child should read up on as much information about that animal as possible – and there are hundreds of pet care books and websites dedicated to specific types of pets. This book provides a clear and comprehensive guide to the basic care of the most popular types of pet.

Each section follows an easy-to-read format detailing the pet's needs and pointers towards gaining further information, such as joining a club devoted to this type of animal. Details of clubs and animal shows can easily be found in specialist publications and on the internet.

Please enjoy the *Complete Pets Handbook* and find out just how wonderful pets can be. Hopefully, having read about your chosen pet, you will get a pet of your own and enjoy a long and happy association with it.

Happy pet keeping!

CATS

Cats must rate as the most enigmatic of pets, perhaps because, unlike dogs, it's very hard to tell what a cat is thinking. Their studied display of indifference to all around them – including humans – has led to cats being ascribed with such qualities as regal, aloof, disdainful, calculating and independent – and yet they remain consistently popular pets. In the US and Australia, they rank second place behind dogs, while in the UK they top the pet popularity poll, pushing dogs into second place.

Perhaps the cat's popularity stems from the fact that we humans have to earn its affection and approval. While dogs are eager to please, cats, it seems, prefer that we are eager to please them!

History of domestic cats

The exact origins of the pet cat are not entirely known. Domestic cats are believed to have developed from several species of smaller wild cats. Three species in particular are considered to be the most likely ancestors of our domestic cat, namely: the African wild cat, the Forest wild cat and the Jungle cat.

The Forest wild cat is closely related to the African wild cat and is found all over Europe. Ancient Egyptians domesticated the Jungle cat as far back as 2000BC. Over the centuries, humans domesticated all of these species and it is believed that the different species were interbred with each other, resulting in a mixture that eventually became the common domestic cat, *Felis catus*.

The Ancient Egyptians were the first to keep cats as pets. This was probably due to the cat's qualities as a rat and mouse catcher. Egyptian tomb paintings, from *circa* 2000BC, depict cats that appear to be accompanying humans in hunting expeditions, much like dogs.

CATS

Later in Egypt, cats were even worshipped as gods and were sometimes believed to be re-incarnations of dead priests. The most famous of these cats was Bast (also known as Bastet), the Egyptian goddess with the head of a cat on a woman's body. Bast was the goddess of fertility and as such she attracted a large cult around her. Bast's popularity undoubtedly had a lot to do with why the Egyptians liked cats. They liked them so much that when a cat died, it would be treated the same way as a dead human being of similar importance and was embalmed and mummified. Cat mummies can be seen in museums today.

In 30BC, Roman legions conquered Cleopatra's Egypt and this led to the domesticated cat spreading to other parts of the world, as many cats were taken away from Egypt by Roman legionnaires. However, during the Middle Ages, particularly in Europe, cats were seen in quite a different light. The church was campaigning against witchcraft and cats became seen as agents of the devil or associates of witches. Consequently, they became hunted and feared.

Once the witch-hunting frenzy started to die out, people realised that cats were useful animals to keep as rat and mouse catchers. By the 18th century people once again began keeping cats simply as pets inside their own homes, although this was mainly the preserve of the upper classes – the lower orders kept cats as working animals, which had to earn their keep by killing rodents.

There are many ways of acquiring a cat or kitten, as there are always large numbers of unwanted cats in rescue shelters

Acquiring a cat

There are many ways of acquiring a cat or kitten, as there are always large numbers of unwanted cats in rescue shelters in need of good homes. Most of these cats are moggies, ie cats of no particular breeding or ancestry. To make sure that you do not unwittingly add to the problem of unwanted cats, please consider carefully whether you really do want a cat and are prepared to look after it for the full length of its life. Cats normally live for at least 12 years, with some reaching ages as great as 20 or even more.

CATS

Cats are independent animals, but that does not mean that they can look after themselves all the time! All cats need feeding, grooming, vaccinations and possibly other veterinary care. If you have an indoor cat it will need a litter tray that will need frequent cleaning. Have you considered what to do when you go on holiday? Does everyone in your family want a cat and are you sure there are no allergies that may prevent you from keeping a cat? Do you have other pets that may be a problem if you get a cat? Dogs and cats normally learn to get on just fine, contrary to popular belief, but if you have a small pet bird such as a budgie, or a pet hamster, you obviously cannot allow a cat anywhere near it.

Moggy or pedigree?

Unlike with dogs, the great majority of cats are randomly bred moggies and most people would probably never even consider a pure-bred, pedigree cat when deciding to acquire a cat as a pet. Moggies do make wonderful pets, but don't forget that there are also many pedigree breeds to choose from. Read books on the different breeds, take a look at specialist magazines or breed websites to find out if there is a particular one that may suit you and your lifestyle best or maybe even visit a cat show. You will also get to meet moggies in the pet classes at cat shows, so you can see the best of both worlds.

A superior white moggy: a moggy makes a wonderful pet and can be just as beautiful as a pedigree

Cats are independent animals, but that does not mean that they can look after themselves all the time!

Those that opt for a pedigree cat often do so because there is a particular trait they would like to see in their cat. For instance, Persians are usually very friendly and laid back; Siamese lively, intelligent and mischievous; and Maine Coons are large, with outgoing temperaments. With a moggy you will never know quite how the cat will turn out and these intelligent cats are often more independent than their pedigree counterparts. For many people, this is the charm of the moggy, for others it is what makes them choose a pedigree breed.

CATS

Reputable cat breeders agree to sell kittens that are at least 13 weeks old and fully vaccinated

Where to find a kitten

If you are looking for a moggy, be it a kitten or an adult cat, do go along to your local cat shelter. These always have many cats in need of good homes, cats that may have to be put to sleep if no home is found. Normally cats from shelters will have been veterinary checked and, if not already neutered, you will be given a voucher for free or discounted neutering. Don't overlook the adult cats! Most people fall for the charm of a little kitten and the adults may be overlooked. Yet an adult cat can still turn out to be a wonderful pet.

There are of course kittens available free or cheaply, for example, via newspaper adverts. Bear in mind when acquiring a moggy kitten that it should ideally be 12 weeks old. Most moggies are given away or sold much younger, but try to avoid people that are giving away kittens aged just five or six weeks, as these will not be old enough to leave their mothers yet.

To find a pedigree breeder of the breed of your choice, there are various cat magazines that list extensive breeders' registers and many breeders also have websites on the internet. Again you can meet breeders by visiting a show. If you contact your country's main cat registry, they will no doubt be able to supply you with a list of forthcoming shows and a list of cat breed clubs for the breed you are interested in. In turn, these breed clubs will be able to put you in touch with good breeders. Be sure to pick a caring, responsible breeder rather than somebody just turning out kittens to make money. You may have to go on a waiting list for the kitten of your dreams from a good breeder. Cat breeders are not pet shops, they breed as a hobby, and will not always have kittens available. All reputable cat breeders agree to sell only kittens that are at least 13 weeks old and fully vaccinated, and a good breeder will want to ask you a lot of questions to ensure you offer a suitable home for their kitten.

If you want to own a pedigree kitten or cat, be sure to pick a caring, responsible breeder

CATS

Male or female?

The best advice here is to go for the kitten you like best and not be overly influenced by its sex. Obviously, if you have visions of breeding pedigree cats, then you need to choose a female, but, if you simply want a pet, then sex shouldn't need to matter at all. Both sexes make equally good pets when neutered. Some pedigree breeders sell their pet kittens already neutered, others will ask you to sign a contract promising to have the kitten neutered before a certain age.

One or two cats?

If you have no other cats, then you should seriously consider getting two kittens as opposed to one, especially if you are out at work during the day. Cats can be very sociable and many do not like to be on their own. Most cats greatly enjoy the company of other cats and, although two cats will mean twice as much feeding and grooming, they will also mean twice as much fun and will always have each other for company. Two cats will not be less affectionate towards their owner than a single cat.

Bringing your new kitten home

Make sure you have a good quality, secure cat carrier to transport the kitten or cat – definitely not just a cardboard box. The carrier should be lined with a comfortable blanket. If you have acquired a pedigree kitten, the breeder should have given you details of what the kitten is used to eating and, ideally, a small amount of food, so that you can continue with the diet that the kitten has been accustomed to. If you intend to change the food to a different brand, it is important to do so gradually to avoid stomach upsets.

When arriving home with the kitten, place the carrier in a quiet spot, open the door and allow the kitten to wander out when it feels ready to explore. Allow it some time to look around its new home and show it where the litter tray and food bowls are kept. If there are other pets in the house, introduce

ACCESSORIES CHECK LIST

- Food
- Cat carrier
- Litter tray and litter
- Food and water bowls
- Brush and comb
- Nail clipper
- Scratching post
- Toys
- Flea treatment
- Worming tablets

CATS

them carefully. Never force the kitten upon an existing pet and never leave a new kitten alone with a dog until you know that they have made friends. A nervous kitten is best kept in one single room to start with, until it has gained the confidence to venture further. Most kittens will settle down almost immediately, but allow up to a week for the newcomer to get used to everything; after all, the kitten has only just left its mother and litter-mates and will naturally feel a bit confused. An adult cat will take longer to settle, especially if nervous. Do allow it plenty of time and wait for the cat to approach you.

Vaccinations

Pedigree kittens will be fully vaccinated when bought, but a moggy kitten will need to see the vet at nine weeks for its first vaccination. All cats need to be protected from incurable, often fatal diseases, whether they are allowed outdoors or stay indoors permanently. Many diseases that are vaccinated against are viral in origin and can be brought into the house simply by means of the cat's owner or a visitor having unwittingly walked through an infected area and then bringing the virus into the house on their shoes.

All cats should be vaccinated against Feline Infectious Enteritis (FIE, also known as Feline Parvovirus) and the two different strains of Feline Influenza, commonly known as Cat Flu. Cats affected with FIE seldom survive and the mortality rate among cats affected by Cat Flu is also high – affected cats that survive may have lasting problems afterwards or indeed become permanent carriers of the disease. Unless your cat is vaccinated, you will not be able to take part in cat shows, nor be able to board your cat in a cattery if you go on holiday. A vet's certificate is required as proof of vaccination. Following their first vaccination at the age of nine weeks (no younger, as they will still have natural immunity from their mother up to this age), a second injection will be needed three weeks later.

All cats need to be protected from incurable, often fatal diseases, whether they are indoor or outdoor cats

CATS

In the US, many states have a law that cats and dogs must be vaccinated against at least some diseases. Check with your vet what requirements apply to where you live. In the UK, you need to have your cat vaccinated against rabies if you ever want to travel abroad with it. Ask your vet for details about the Pets Passport scheme.

It is also possible to vaccinate against Feline Leukaemia Virus (FeLV), another infectious disease that is incurable and always fatal. These days, the FeLV vaccine can be given at the same time as the one for FIE and Cat Flu. Many breeders vaccinate against FeLV, although by no means all. Unlike FIE and Cat Flu, FeLV cannot be transmitted easily without the cat having had close contact with an infected cat (such as fighting, mating, mutual grooming or sharing food bowls) and, as breeders regularly test their cats for FeLV, it follows that an indoor cat in a FeLV negative household runs little or no risk of ever being infected with FeLV.

FeLV vaccination should, however, always be considered for cats that are allowed to go out. Before being vaccinated against FeLV, the cat should be blood-tested to ensure that it hasn't already been infected, as an infected cat may appear healthy for quite some time, sometimes even years.

Discuss your cat with your vet to decide what you should or should not vaccinate against

Feline Chlamydia is another viral disease for which a vaccine is available, but which isn't given routinely, nor required at shows. Chlamydia, which causes sneezing and severe eye infection, can be a real nuisance and is difficult to eradicate once encountered, but it is not fatal. In the US, there are also vaccines against Feline Immunodeficiency Virus (FIV) and Feline Infectious Peritonitis (FIP). Both have received mixed reports as to their actual effectiveness. Discuss your cat with your vet to decide what you should or should not vaccinate against.

Pedigree kittens will be fully vaccinated when bought, but a moggy kitten will need to see the vet at nine weeks for its first vaccination

Annual boosters are needed to keep the cat's immunity up to date and your vet can also provide you with details of this.

CATS

Neutering

Any cat, of whatever breed, which is not specifically intended for breeding, should be neutered. All moggies should be neutered, as there are already many thousands of unwanted cats in need of good homes without more kittens being added to the population needlessly. To leave a non-breeding cat entire, as it is known, isn't only impractical, it is unkind to the cat.

A male cat that is left entire will be frustrated by the lack of females to mate with and it will also be likely to spray urine all over its living quarters (including your house and its furniture!) to mark its territory. Its urine will also smell very strongly, even if confined to the litter tray. A neutered male cat will be far more relaxed than an entire male, and so will make a much better pet. If you have other cats, neutering is essential: not only does it prevent unwanted/unplanned litters from being born, it also ensures that the cats get on better with each other, as males are unlikely to stay friendly towards each other unless neutered.

Needless to say, no entire male (or female) cat should ever be allowed outdoor access, as it will mate with any female that it comes across and will fight with other entire males. It will also be at great risk from getting infected by diseases spread via mating and fighting, such as FeLV or FIV (see Vaccinations above).

Likewise, female cats not intended for breeding should be neutered. An entire female will come into season ('call') on a regular basis, particularly during the spring or summer. When living indoors in a centrally heated house, it may well come into call all year round. If it does, it will scream loudly for up to a week, trying to attract males. It too may spray urine or urinate on your carpets and may lose its appetite, therefore losing weight and condition in the long run. Unless mated, it will continue to call and its calls will gradually last longer and longer, until eventually it may have one continuous call that simply does not stop unless she is mated or neutered ('spayed', as the term is known as in females). A queen that is allowed to

A healthy cat is a happy cat

CATS

call for too long may also develop fallopian cysts or other medical problems.

Neutering doesn't change your cat's personality and it does not make it put on a lot of weight unless you overfeed it.

It is possible to put a female cat on the contraceptive pill or to give it contraceptive injections. However, all medical interference with hormones can cause problems and a much safer and permanent solution is to have the cat neutered.

Neutering is not a major operation in cats, unlike in many other animals. A male cat will be back to its normal self within hours, with no stitches, and a female will normally only have two or three stitches, either in its side or in its belly, to be removed after seven to ten days. It will, therefore, take the female a few days to recover from the operation and you will need to make sure that it does not chew at her stitches in an attempt to remove them – if it does, it will need to be fitted with an Elizabethan collar, which your vet can supply. However, most cats tend to leave their stitches alone.

Discuss with your vet the best age at which to have your cat neutered as opinions vary between vets.

Feeding

To a certain extent, it can be argued that feeding a cat these days only involves opening a can or a packet of food. However, it is important that your cat gets exactly what it needs – and dietary needs vary between individual cats depending on age, whether neutered or not, or whether breeding or non-breeding.

Cats are obligate carnivores, which means that they need meat to be able to survive

But is commercial cat food really necessary? Surely moggies have for years managed to survive without expensive shop-bought food, being fed leftovers instead? The answer is yes, commercial food is necessary (unless you feed it a special natural raw meat diet which requires some expert knowledge – ask your vet for advice), as the moggies of yesteryear, which managed to

CATS

You will seldom go wrong if you feed your kitten on the diet that the breeder has reared it on

survive on a diet of the family's leftover porridge and the like, went hunting to supplement their diet with rats and mice.

Cats are obligate carnivores, which means that they need meat to be able to survive (unlike dogs, which are omnivorous and can survive on a vegetarian diet), and therefore they require a large amount of protein in their diet to be able to stay healthy. It is very difficult to feed a cat on a home-cooked diet, while ensuring that it does not lack any essential nutrients.

Cats also need a diet high in fat as well as protein. Their intestines are constructed for this type of diet, which means that the cat will be provided with as much energy as possible without the need for excessive bulk.

Cats have no specific need for carbohydrates, but these can still be found in some commercial cat foods in the form of cereal. This is a cheap and inferior source of energy, which lacks some of the amino acids that are essential to cats. Therefore, cat foods that contain cereal in anything but very small amounts should be avoided.

If you are new to cats and have just purchased your first pedigree kitten, it is strongly recommended that you take your kitten's breeder's advice on feeding. Breeders that have been keeping and rearing their chosen breed for several years will have a lot of experience of what their cats thrive on, so you will seldom go wrong if you follow their advice. A good breeder will normally give you a diet sheet, detailing what food your kitten has been used to, the frequency of feeding etc. Many breeders will also provide you with a small amount of that food to tide you over for a few days, until you have had a chance to purchase some yourself.

If your cat is a rescued moggy, your vet will of course be able to advise you on feeding

If your cat is a rescued moggy, your vet will of course be able to advise you on feeding.

One of the first questions that most new cat owners will want an answer to is whether to feed canned food, dry food or a combination of both. The main difference between canned and dry food is the water content. A can of cat food contains

CATS

a minimum of 75% water, often 80%. Dry food contains a maximum of 12% water. Both have their advantages and disadvantages. When eating canned food, the cat will automatically ingest a large amount of water, whereas, if fed on dry food, it is essential that the cat drinks water to stay healthy. Water is the cat's single most important nutrient. A cat denied water will die of dehydration much sooner than it would die of starvation if denied food. In addition, without enough water the cat's urine will become concentrated and this can cause urological problems.

Dry food is of course more concentrated than canned food, so the cat needs to eat less of it than of any canned food. It also takes up less storage space and is usually more economical to feed than canned food. Dry food helps the cat to keep its teeth well exercised due to its crunchy texture, although feeding a dry diet is by no means any guarantee of your cat always having clean, tartar-free teeth.

A good solution is to feed a mixture of canned and dry food – one meal of each per day for adult cats.

Whether fed on canned or dry food, your cat should always have water available. Many cats fed solely on a diet of canned food will almost never be seen to drink, but the water needs to be available just in case. Cats fed on a dry diet will normally drink a good amount each day. It is a good idea to use a pet drinking fountain which serves running, filtered water to encourage your cat to drink.

Water is the liquid to offer your cat – not milk or cream. Kittens should be allowed to suckle their mothers for at least 10 weeks and so will need no supplementary feeding with milk. Milk should not be seen as a drink as such, it is food to a cat. Also, most adult cats' sensitive digestive systems will not tolerate milk, so any milk given, be it ordinary cow's milk or milk specifically intended for cats (including ready-mixed milk for adult cats), will usually cause diarrhoea.

Kittens have very small stomachs, yet they require as much as three times the energy levels required for an adult cat, so it is

CATS

WHY IS MY CAT NOT USING ITS LITTER TRAY?

- Does its litter tray need changing? Cats will not use the tray if it is not changed regularly.

- Is your cat's food situated too close to its litter tray? Cats don't like to mess where they eat.

- If your cat messes in an unsuitable place, try placing food bowls there or sprinkle pieces of dry food in the area.

- Have you recently changed the brand of cat litter you use? Some cats will only use the brand they are used to.

- Have your cat checked by a vet – improper urination could be a sign of illness such as cystitis.

- Is your cat adult and sexually mature but not neutered? Neutering often helps solve house-training issues.

essential to feed kittens on a diet specifically formulated for growing kittens. If a kitten is fed on food intended for adult cats, it would need to eat very large amounts to be able to gain all the nutrients required to grow and develop properly and, as its stomach is so small, the kitten will be physically unable to do so. The kitten may feel full up, but will instead eventually start to suffer from dietary deficiencies.

Kittens are normally weaned aged four to five weeks – although this does not mean that they should be taken away from their mother at that age, it simply means that this is the age to start offering meals of solid food as a supplement to their mother's milk. From the age of 13 weeks, which is when a pedigree kitten will be sold, a kitten will need four meals per day. By five to six months (depending on the size of the kitten) this can be dropped to three meals and, once adult (aged nine months), the cat will normally require just two meals a day.

Cats are very good at manipulating their owners and many cats manage to 'train' their owners to feed them only their very favourite food, whatever this may be. The cat will simply refuse to eat anything but the preferred food, which may not be a good idea in the long run, especially if the food in question isn't what is best for your cat. There is no need to let your cat dictate feeding like this. If your cat refuses the food you choose, simply take it away and offer the same food again at the next meal. No cat will starve itself to death and all cats will eventually start to eat what is on offer when they realise that going hungry will not make a better alternative appear.

Day-to-day care

All cats will of course need feeding daily. If your cat is living indoors, it will need its litter tray cleaned regularly too. Cats are very clean animals and if they have no clean litter tray available to use, they may decide to use your carpet as a toilet instead!

Cats will also need regular grooming, but just how frequent this should be will vary greatly from cat to cat. For instance, a

CATS

Siamese will have a very short, close laying coat that will only need the occasional quick grooming session with a rubber brush perhaps once a week – more when shedding old fur. A Burmese or other semi-longhaired cat will need combing and brushing a couple of times a week, whereas the true longhaired cats, the Persians, need daily combing and brushing to keep the coat free from tangles.

Flea prevention

No cat needs to suffer from flea infestations these days with so many excellent preventatives available to keep your cat flea-free for several months at a time. There are long-lasting sprays, drops to be put onto the cat's neck, tablets to be given with food once a month or even injections. Talk to your vet about what is available. Items such as flea powder or flea collars purchased from pet shops or grocery stores are usually less effective than those sold by vets. The flea treatments available from vets are more expensive, but they will keep your cat flea-free and are also safe to use. Always seek the advice of your vet if using any products on kittens.

Worming

If your cat has outdoor access, or if it has had fleas, this will increase the risk of it catching worms that live in its digestive system. De-worm on a regular basis with a quality worming treatment supplied by your vet and do ask for advice on when to worm and what to use against what types of worm, as this may vary between countries.

Cats that are indoors only and flea-free do not normally require regular worming, but again ask your vet for advice.

All cats need feeding, grooming, vaccinations and veterinary care

No cat needs to suffer from flea infestations these days with so many excellent preventatives available

CATS

If your cat is to spend time outdoors, make sure it is microchipped

Ears

Your cat's ears may need occasional attention – especially if your cat is longhaired and has a lot of fur inside its ears. The long hair keeps their ears warm, but also makes them produce more wax. Check the ears of your cat regularly and if there is a build up of wax (a greasy, grey-brown substance) simply wipe this away using a dry piece of cotton wool or special ear wipe. No cleaning fluid should be necessary as long as the substance inside the ears is only wax and not an infection of any sort (such as a yeast infection or ear mites – both will be dark brown, almost black in colour). Do not use cotton tops to clean inside the ear – it is quite enough to just wipe clean the outer ear. If a healthy ear is disturbed too much, the wax production may be stimulated unnecessarily and will cause the cat problems.

Claws

The claws of your cat do not normally require a lot of attention. However, as your cat grows older, you may find that the claws thicken and grow longer than normal, in which case regular trimming of the claws will be necessary. For younger cats, this isn't usually necessary, although if you find that you get accidentally scratched when playing with your cat, regular trimming can be a good idea. Trimming of the claws may not help to save your furniture from wear and tear if it is being used as a scratching post by the cat: once you have trimmed the cat's claws, it may instead feel that some extra exercise on your furniture is just what the claws need. Far better then to get the cat used to using a scratching post from an early age.

De-clawing is banned in most countries except the US and involves the actual amputation of the cat's first toe joint. This will render the cat unable to climb properly and is not a procedure to recommend.

CATS

Indoor or outdoor cat?

Whether your cat should be an indoor cat only or have access to the great outdoors is an issue which needs very serious consideration. It is also an issue where people often disagree. In the UK, most cat shelters will not re-home a cat unless it will be allowed to go outside; in the US, most will not re-home a cat unless it will not be allowed out!

There is much to be said for keeping a cat indoors. Consider this: a cat that is allowed outdoor access will also be able to have close contact with other cats, including strays. Even cats that look perfectly healthy may be disease carriers and so your cat could get infected with, for instance, Feline Leukaemia Virus (FeLV), although it is possible to vaccinate against this; Feline Infectious Anemia (FIA, or Haemobartonella), which is spread by fleas and affects a cat who hasn't recently been treated with effective flea preventatives; or Feline Immunodeficiency Virus (FIV), for which there is no reliable preventative or cure.

A cat that is allowed outdoor access may be run over by a car, attacked by a dog, be stolen or get lost – or have any number of accidents.

A cat which is allowed outdoor access may well kill and eat wildlife such as mice, voles and small birds – which more than likely will infect the cat with worms.

If you really would like your cat to be able to spend some time outdoors, we would strongly recommend either a very well fenced and netted-in garden (to stop your cat from getting out and others from getting in) or why not an enclosed garden run where your cat can spend sunny days?

If your cat is to spend time outdoors, make sure it is microchipped, as this will give it a much better chance of being re-united with you should it become lost.

To avoid your cat scratching and damaging your furniture, carpets and walls, supply it with a scratching post from day one

CATS

Training

Unless you are a specialist animal trainer, working for television or in a circus, you will find it is more or less impossible to train a cat. Cats are such independent animals that they will not allow anybody to be in charge of them – unlike dogs who are happiest when a human is their boss.

For an indoor cat, the most important lesson for them to learn is to be clean in the house. Thankfully, this is normally a very easy task with cats. Little or no training is needed, as the cat will understand what to do once it is shown the litter tray. Make sure your new kitten or cat is shown where the litter tray is and that this is not too close to where it eats: cats do not like to go to toilet in the same place as they eat. The rest normally follows naturally.

To avoid your cat scratching and damaging your furniture, carpets and walls, supply it with a scratching post from day one. Many different types are available from pet shops, from simple sisal rope-covered posts to elaborate climbing frames. Most cats will use these if they are available – especially if they are treated with catnip. Should your cat attempt to scratch elsewhere, squirt it with a water pistol! The cat will soon associate an unpleasant soaking with scratching somewhere that is off-limits. Do make sure that an adult is in charge of this procedure.

Showing

Showing your cat can be great fun and you do not even need to own a pedigree cat. Most cat organisations hold classes for household pet cats within their shows and these are judged on their temperament and condition only, so any pet cat that is in excellent condition and is friendly and outgoing has a chance to win. Exactly what rules apply will vary from country to country and between the different organisations. Some only accept moggies to be shown as household pets, others accept pedigree cats too – as long as these are not shown in the pedigree section as well.

CATS

Pedigree cats are judged on their looks alone (although they must of course still be healthy and easy to handle) and each breed has a written standard of points which describe the ideal way for that breed to look. Coat, colour, eye colour, shape of body and face are all taken into account.

If you want to show your pedigree cat, it needs to be registered in your name with the relevant registry organisation. Talk to your cat's breeder for advice, as he or she will be best placed to help you out and tell you whether your cat is a potential champion or not.

Pedigree cats sold as pets only are usually sold as such because they have some small beauty defect which does not make the cat less suitable as a pet, but which may make it unsuitable for showing.

At cat shows, the cats need to be caged for the day and sometimes for a whole weekend. If you would like to show your cat, it is a good idea to get it used to being kept in a cage before the show (such as a medium-size dog crate) so that you know the experience will not worry it.

Contact one of your country's cat registries for help and advice on how to get started with showing. Rules vary a lot between different countries.

A Persian cat: only pedigree cats should be used for breeding

Breeding

Only pedigree cats should be used for breeding; this cannot be stressed enough. The world is full of unwanted cats and kittens, many thousands of which have to be put to sleep each year because suitable homes cannot be found for them. The great majority of these cats are moggies. For some reason, the humble moggy is seen as of little value and something which can be discarded when the novelty of a new pet has worn off.

People who do not neuter their cats and then allow them to go outside give rise to the birth of many unplanned litters of kittens.

CATS

If you are breeding cats, you will need to find good quality, breeding animals

The moggy as such will not die out if not used for breeding. There will always be more moggies, as there will always be irresponsible people about, allowing their cats to breed. There is no need whatsoever to deliberately breed a litter of moggy kittens. Even if you want to keep a kitten yourself or have friends that want a kitten, would it not be better to go along to a shelter and pick a cat that may otherwise be put to sleep?

Responsible breeders that breed pedigree cats as a hobby, for showing, are not adding to the problem of unwanted cats. These breeders make sure suitable homes are found and the people who have decided they want to own a cat of a certain breed due to its particular characteristics are very unlikely to want to acquire a moggy instead.

If you want to breed pedigree cats, consider it all very carefully. You will need good quality, breeding animals that will cost a lot to buy, far more than the cost of ordinary kittens. Selling pedigree kittens isn't always easy and those breeders that do well at shows, and are known to be responsible and caring, will often be approached first. Novice breeders sometimes find it hard to sell their kittens simply because they are not yet well known within the pedigree cat world. As such you may end up having to keep an entire litter of kittens.

Health testing is very important when breeding pedigree cats. Many breeds suffer from hereditary problems and potential breeding cats should be tested before being used for breeding, such as Persians and exotics that need to test negative for Polycystic Kidney Disease. Naturally, you will only want to produce happy, healthy kittens that can live long lives.

You will find a lot of rewards in breeding cats, but not financial ones

You need to find out whether there is a stud male owned by another breeder that you can pay to use or whether you will have to buy your own stud. If you have to buy your own, it will involve you building it separate quarters, as it cannot be allowed to live indoors and mix with your other cats because it will spray urine and will mate every female in call. You will probably have to have your female (queen) blood-tested to prove that it is free of diseases such as FeLV and FIV before taking it to stud.

Pedigree queens often end up needing emergency caesarians or

GROOMING HINTS AND TIPS

- Use a rubber, bristled brush for grooming your very short-coated cat once a week
- Use a metal, moulting comb and slicker brush for grooming your thick-coated short-hair or semi-longhair twice a week
- Use a metal, moulting comb and slicker brush to groom your Persian every day
- Sprinkle baby talcum powder into your long haired cat's coat before grooming to get rid of excess grease and dirt
- Use special ear wipes to remove excess wax from your cat's ears
- Use saline solution on cotton wool if you need to clean around your cat's eyes
- If your cat is very dirty or its coat seems greasy and mats easily, a bath may be needed
- If your cat objects to being groomed, clip his or her claws first to avoid being scratched
- Small specks of black dirt in your cat's coat indicate fleas. Use a flea comb and obtain flea treatment from your vet.

other veterinary care, and this incurs a great cost – especially if it should happen at night. You may have to hand-rear your kittens day and night, if the mother does not want to know them or if she does not have enough milk. The kittens need to be kept for 13 weeks and should be vaccinated, registered, preferably microchipped and insured.

You will need to find suitable homes for them and ensure potential buyers are responsible – and agree to take the cat back if the new owner cannot keep it. All in all, this makes for a lot of hard work and a lot of expense.

Of course, you will also find a lot of rewards in breeding cats, but not financial ones – please do not think that it will earn you any money, as quite simply it will not. Read specialist books, talk to breeders and more than anything discuss any potential breeding plans with your cat's breeder.

Cats, worshipped by the Ancient Egyptians, are the most loveable and rewarding of pets.

Health testing is very important when breeding pedigree cats

DOGS

Dogs are, without a doubt, not only great pets, but also valuable working animals. Everyone will have heard the phrase 'man's best friend', but they are far more than that. They are more our partners – and this partnership stretches back to the dawn of human civilisation.

History of dogs

It is widely known that our domestic pet dogs are descended from wolves. Experts disagree, however, on just how long ago humans first started keeping dogs as pets. A controversial new study suggests that dogs were domesticated more than 100,000 years ago. However, the most commonly held belief is that dogs were domesticated after *circa* 10,000BC. Furthermore, it is only comparatively recently that different breeds of dogs have started to appear.

Originally, all dogs looked much the same, rather wolf-like, until we started to breed dogs selectively. It is hard to believe today that a yorkshire terrier and a Saint Bernard are both descended from wolves. Dogs now come in more than 300 different breeds worldwide and the differences between certain breeds can be very pronounced.

No doubt early humans had no intention of creating breeds of dogs that looked so vastly different to each other. However, they discovered that, if you selected animals for their particular attributes, you were able to combine all the qualities that were sought after in one dog. Initially these would have been qualities such as guarding, hunting and herding.

All breeds were created with a specific purpose in mind. The various collie breeds were bred to herd sheep. Retriever breeds, spaniels and even poodles were all bred to be gundogs. Many terriers were bred to hunt vermin. Even a pure pet breed such as the Cavalier King Charles spaniel, favoured by royalty and bred to be the companions of the rich and titled, were bred with an intention – to attract fleas that might otherwise prefer to settle on humans.

DOGS

Each year many thousands of dogs end up in rescue centres as unwanted

Today, most dogs are kept mainly as pets, although many still work, such as sheepdogs, police dogs and guide dogs. Breeds that were originally developed for a very specific purpose may no longer have any other role to fulfil than as a pet in modern society. But the original characteristics, selectively bred for many years, often still exist in these dogs: a golden retriever will still have an inborn wish to retrieve and a border collie will want to herd its flock.

Acquiring a dog

Before you even ask yourself 'What kind of dog should I get?' or 'Where can I find a puppy?', it is essential to carefully consider if your circumstances allow you to keep a dog and if you are prepared for all the hard work that owning a dog entails. Dogs don't necessarily arrive already house-trained, nor do they necessarily respond to basic commands. Each year many thousands of dogs end up in rescue centres as unwanted and many of these ultimately end up being put to sleep. In the great majority of cases, the situation could have been avoided had the owners spent more time considering whether they were suitable as dog owners.

So, first of all ask yourself the following questions:

- Are you prepared to look after a dog for all of its life? The life span of a dog is normally 12 to 15 years.

- Have you got the time necessary to spend with a dog? Every dog, regardless of breed and size, will need regular exercise and training, as well as grooming.

- Is there somebody at home during most of the day, who is able to look after the dog? It is never a good idea to leave a dog alone for more than a few hours each day. Dogs are pack animals that need companionship, but having two dogs instead of one is no substitute for human companionship. Somebody must be able to walk the dog at regular intervals. If you leave your dog alone all day, you will most likely return home each day to a soiled and messy house. You could leave your dog outside in a

DOGS

kennel, but it may bark and annoy your neighbours. A puppy cannot be left alone at all until it gets older.

- **Does everyone in your family want a dog?** A dog is a family member and needs to be wanted by everyone. Even if one family member agrees to be responsible for the dog's care, there will be times when someone else will need to help out. And an adult, rather than a child, should have ultimate responsibility for the dog's welfare.

- **Can you afford to care for a dog?** The purchase price is a minor point when you compare it to the costs of food, vaccinations and other veterinary care. A large dog will naturally cost more to feed than a small one. There will also be the initial outlay for equipment such as a bed, collars, leads and toys. Consider taking out pet insurance to help offset the cost of unexpected veterinary bills.

You must be prepared to take your dog for walks at least five times a day, regardless of the weather

- **Is your home suitable for a dog?** If you rent you may be prohibited from keeping pets. Ideally, anyone considering owning a dog needs to live in a house with a securely fenced-in back garden. This will make life a lot easier for you when it comes to allowing your dog to perform its natural functions. Many rescue societies will not consider homing a dog with a person living in a flat, nor will most breeders. However, if you are committed to owning a dog, living in a flat should not necessarily prevent you from doing so as long as you are prepared to take the dog outside for walks at least five times a day, every day, regardless of the weather. You will also need to consider the size of your home when choosing a dog. You do not want a giant breed in a tiny home.

It is essential to carefully consider whether your circumstances allow you to keep a dog

- **Have you considered what to do with the dog if you want to go on holiday?** Many dogs end up being dumped at rescue kennels when their owners go on holiday. This is often because the owners had not made arrangements in advance for someone to look after their dog.

- **Finally, are you pregnant and considering starting a family sometime in the future?** You need to consider whether you

DOGS

will be able to spend time with your dog once you have a demanding newborn baby or toddler. Likewise, if you are elderly you need to consider whether you will still be fit enough to walk a dog in years to come. Consider your circumstances and whether an adult dog might be a better choice than a puppy.

Which breed of dog suits you?

Having decided that you are prepared to look after a dog for all of its life, your next question should be which breed of dog to choose. This is not simply a question of picking a breed of dog that appeals to you because of its appearance. Many dog owners do not do enough research about the breeds before choosing a dog. Not every breed is suitable for everyone. There are hundreds of breeds to choose from, as well as crossbreeds and mongrels, and the decision as to what dog to choose is a very important one.

There are hundreds of breeds to choose from, as well as crossbreeds and mongrels

Read books about dog breeds. Ask other dog owners for advice. Visit dog shows and view the different breeds there. Here you can meet dogs of more or less every Kennel Club recognised breed. There are also various dog magazines and newspapers that have excellent articles on individual breeds and their care.

Consider the size of your prospective pet – a very small dog may not be suitable for you

Size and coat

Consider the size of dog. Do you want a small, medium, large or giant breed of dog? All dogs need the same care and basic training, but a larger dog will cost more to feed and the giant breeds generally have a shorter life span than the toy breeds. A large dog may be harder for a young or old person to control than a small one, but a very small dog may not be suitable in a home where there are very young children who may pick the dog up and drop it. The dog's coat is also an important consideration. Some breeds need daily brushing and combing to prevent them getting matted and dirty. Others need

DOGS

professional grooming such as clipping or trimming. Some are smooth coated and therefore need very little coat care.

Temperament and training

The dog's temperament is important to consider. Do you want a dog that is friendly towards strangers? Would you prefer one that will guard your home? Do you want to spend half an hour a day on walks and training, or three hours? If you want a dog that needs the minimum amount of walks, it would be disastrous to acquire a border collie or German shepherd, for instance, as they are high energy dogs that need a lot of exercise and training to be happy. A frustrated dog soon becomes a problem dog. Likewise, if you are happy to spend a lot of time hiking outdoors, you would be unwise to choose a bulldog or Saint Bernard, which are more sedate breeds happy with shorter walks.

The ease of training is also something that varies a lot between different breeds. Some breeds are known to be easy to train and particularly suitable for novice dog owners, others can be stubborn and require more experienced owners.

Origins

When choosing a breed, do bear in mind the dog's original role. Collies and shepherds, for instance, often feel happiest when given some form of work to do (obedience training can constitute 'work') and they may want to herd their flock – even if that flock consists of your children and not sheep. Retrievers will carry items around in their mouths. Terriers will often hunt small animals. Exceptions exist, but it helps a great deal if you have a fair idea of what to expect from a particular breed. You will not, then, be surprised when you find your golden retriever carrying the TV remote control in its mouth or when your Newfoundland jumps into the village pond for a swim at every opportunity.

New pets can give you hours of entertainment!

ACCESSORIES CHECK LIST

- Collar
- Lead
- ID disc for collar
- Pooper scooper or plastic bags
- Bed
- Food and water bowl
- Toys
- Brush and/or comb
- Nail clipper
- Food
- Flea treatment
- Worming tablets

DOGS

'Hybrid vigour'

There are many mongrels and crossbreeds that can be found in dogs' homes or that are advertised in your local newspapers. Usually these dogs are in need of good homes. Not only would you be doing a good deed by taking one of them on, a mongrel could turn out to be your perfect dog. However, do bear in mind that mongrels are randomly bred and this means it is difficult to predict what they will be like both in temperament and size. Often it is possible to detect certain ancestry in a mongrel. If it does resemble a particular breed then you will have some idea of how your dog may turn out. With a pedigree breed you can be pretty certain of your future dog's traits. So, if you definitely want a dog that, for instance, will welcome any stranger into your home with a wagging tail, then you may be safer opting for a pedigree dog.

It is not necessarily true to say that mongrels are healthier than pedigree dogs because of so-called 'hybrid vigour'. Randomly bred dogs may be just as inbred, if not more so, than pedigree dogs. Who is to say the mongrel puppy you see was not the result of a mating between a brother and a sister? Likewise mongrels can suffer from the same hereditary ailments that affect some pedigree dogs.

Dog or bitch? What age?

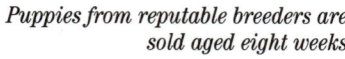

Puppies from reputable breeders are sold aged eight weeks

Whether you choose a dog or a bitch as a pet is a personal choice. Some people prefer dogs, others prefer bitches. Assuming you are looking for a pet dog and not one for breeding, you should not need to consider the sex too much. Physically, dogs are bigger and stronger than bitches. It would be a good idea to meet both sexes of your chosen breed as this will give you a good idea of what of expect.

Puppies from reputable breeders are sold aged eight weeks. This is an ideal age as the puppy will be ready to leave its mother, yet will still be young enough to settle easily into a new home and to be trained. The older the puppy or dog, the more set in its ways it will be. That is not to say that you cannot train

DOGS

an adult dog. It will just take a little more time. The old saying, 'you cannot teach an old dog new tricks,' is simply not true. Adult dogs may well have formed bad habits that need dealing with, especially if they have been rescued, but this can be done with time, patience and dedication.

Where to buy your dog

It may seem as easy to buy a dog as it is to go out and buy a TV – you just open your local newspaper and pick the advert with the cheapest possible puppies for sale. There are hundreds of dogs for sale at a cheap price. Or you could visit a pet shop that sells dogs, couldn't you? NO. This cannot be stressed enough. If you want to be sure of acquiring a well-bred, properly reared, pedigree dog from healthy parents and with the right temperament for the breed, then your only option is to contact a reputable breeder. You must have proper documentation for your dog, which should detail the relevant health tests of the parents. Therefore, buying a pedigree dog with a pedigree supplied and a Kennel Club registration document is just as important for the average pet buyer as it is for somebody wanting a potential show dog. There are a lot of people out there who breed dogs just to make money. To be able to make money out of breeding puppies, corners have to be cut – usually in the form of the dogs' health – a problem often encountered with dogs bred and sold from puppy farms and puppy mills.

Again, research your chosen breed. The great majority of pedigree breeds do have some hereditary problems. Responsible breeders will take every step possible to make sure that they only breed from healthy dogs. Generally, they spend a lot of money on health-testing their dogs.

Exactly what tests you should expect your puppy's parents to have undergone will depend on the breed. This is why it is so important to know your facts before you buy. For instance, most large breeds should have parents whose hips have been x-rayed (hip scored) and found to be free of hip dysplasia, otherwise your puppy may end up with severe arthritis when older or may even need a hip replacement when young. The eyes of most

The older the puppy or dog, the more set in its ways it will be

DOGS

breeds should have been examined by an eye specialist. Dalmatian puppies should be tested for deafness. Cavalier King Charles spaniels often suffer from heart problems and should be bred from parents that are tested annually. The list goes on. Only by buying a puppy from health-tested parents will you be able to feel reasonably safe that you have bought a healthy puppy.

So, do not buy a puppy from a newspaper advert that states 'no papers' or 'unregistered'. It is inadvisable to buy a puppy from a pet shop, as in many cases these will have been bred in puppy farms from unhealthy bitches, often of unsound temperament, who have been bred from again and again to produce as many puppies as possible. Often puppies in pet shops have been taken from their mothers too early, transported long distances and may well be unhealthy. Instead, find the good breeders. Your Kennel Club can give you a list of breed clubs.

Responsible breeders do not breed just to sell, they mainly breed for a puppy that they can keep back for showing and the ultimate motive is never to make a quick profit. As such, the good breeders may not have puppies as readily available as the irresponsible ones. Therefore, you may find that you need to put your name down on a waiting list for a puppy, especially if it is a less common breed. This should not put you off. You are going to spend at least 10 years with your dog, so what's a wait of a few months if it ensures you get the best possible puppy? Be patient. Do not be tempted to buy the cheap puppy 'without papers' from a newspaper advert rather than waiting for the more expensive Kennel Club registered one from the recommended breeder. The cheaper puppy may end up costing you far more in vet's bills.

If you want a crossbreed or mongrel, do go along to the nearest animal rescue charity or similar. You will also find pedigree dogs there, but these will have an unknown health history, although they should still look and behave like their breed. Most breed clubs also have rescue officers that deal with re-homing their breed. If you would prefer to give a home to an unwanted dog or maybe would prefer an adult rather than a

Dalmatian puppies should be tested for deafness before buying them

DOGS

puppy, but would still like to chose a particular breed, then breed rescue is an excellent alternative.

Do ask the breeder or shelter/rescue as many questions as possible and do expect to be asked a lot of questions in return. All good breeders or rescues will want to make sure that you are a suitable potential owner. You will be asked questions about where you live, who shares your home, your working hours, other pets you might have or previous dog experience. The rescues will often want to do a home check to ensure you have a suitably fenced garden, among other things. Do not feel annoyed by the questions, welcome them and answer them honestly. Anyone who asks a lot of questions will do so because they care about their dogs.

Bringing your new dog home

Pick a quiet time to bring home your new puppy or dog. At all costs avoid noisy family occasions such as Christmas and birthdays. You will find that no reputable breeder or rescue shelter will sell dogs at these times. The dog will be unsure of what to expect in its new home: it may be away from its mother and siblings for the first time, and so calm and quiet are needed. Don't expect miracles – a puppy will not be house-trained and an adult rescue may have accidents for the first few days. Make sure your new dog has a quiet area with a bed in which to sleep and that he or she is shown where the water bowl is. A soft blanket, some toys, a calm atmosphere, some reassurance and hopefully your dog should soon settle in.

A dog is always a loyal companion

A soft blanket, some toys, a calm atmosphere, some reassurance and your dog should soon settle in

Nutrition and feeding

The subject of feeding your dog may seem bewildering to the novice dog owner. There are so many different brands of dog food available from supermarkets, pet shops and vets, and if you ask 10 different people what kind of food is best to feed

DOGS

your dog you will probably get 10 different answers. Therefore, in the first instance, trust the advice of your dog's breeder. They will no doubt have many years' experience of feeding that breed. You should have been given a diet sheet when you bought your puppy, detailing what and when to feed it. If your dog is a rescue, ask your vet for advice if you are unsure of your dog's dietary requirements.

Dogs are omnivores, which means that they eat both meat and other foods – they do not need to live on meat alone. There is a trend these days for natural feeding, that is to feed only raw meaty bones and similar, or home-prepared diets. This can work very well but will require some specialist knowledge, so do ask a vet for advice before embarking on any such diet.

Puppies aged between eight and 12 weeks (approximately) need four or five meals a day. Again, ask the breeder for advice. There are many good complete diets available to buy and many are specifically aimed at puppies (any dog younger than 12 months). However, the puppy diets are rich in protein and may be unsuitable for some dogs, particularly giant breeds such as Saint Bernards, as these need to grow slowly in order to develop strong and healthy bones. The choices available are normally a dry, complete food that needs nothing added to it or canned meat with added mixer biscuits. Both are good choices.

Dogs are omnivores, which means that they do not need to live on meat alone

If you are feeding a dry food, it is always advisable to soak this in warm water for at least half an hour before feeding. This will avoid the situation where the food swells inside the dog's stomach, which can cause indigestion and at times more serious problems such as torsion (twisting of the gut).

At 12 weeks, the number of meals can be reduced to three a day and at around eight months of age your puppy can be fed just twice a day. It is a good idea to continue feeding two meals a day for the rest of the dog's life. If feeding just one meal, you will need to feed twice as much in one meal and large breeds in particular can have a problem with this.

DOGS

Treats are very useful for training your dog and there are a great number of these available in both supermarkets and pet shops. Do remember that these should be just occasional treats. Try to not get into the habit of giving your dog treats just because he or she is begging. If you always make your dog work for a treat, by responding to a simple command such as sitting or fetching a toy, your dog will learn that it has to do something to earn a reward. This will greatly help you train it, while also ensuring that your dog never develops the habit of begging for food.

Vitamins and calcium supplements do not need to be added to complete diets.

Vaccination

Your new puppy will need to be vaccinated, normally between eight and nine weeks, with a second injection around three weeks later. Dogs need to be vaccinated against distemper, parvo, hepatitis and leptospirosis. In some countries, and some states in the US, they also need to be vaccinated against rabies. It is also possible to vaccinate against kennel cough, which is particularly important if your dog is going to spend time with a lot of other dogs, such as in boarding kennels, at shows or in training classes. Vaccinations need to be boosted at regular intervals – ask your vet for advice on this. The diseases we vaccinate against are all very serious, contagious and usually fatal. When you take your dog for its vaccination, be it a puppy for the first time or an adult for its booster, your vet will also give your dog a thorough health examination.

You should also worm your dog four times a year and, again, your vet will have the most effective tablets. If ever in doubt about your dog's health, always see a vet.

Neutering

Whether or not to neuter your dog or spay your bitch is another personal choice. There are both pros and cons to consider.

Vaccinations need to be boosted at regular intervals – ask your vet for advice on this

DOGS

If you only own one dog and ensure it does not stray, there is little risk of unwanted puppies resulting – but if you are in any doubt as to whether your dog or bitch may ever be able to get out and mate (this is why a secure back garden is essential) then you should seriously consider neutering. There are enough unwanted puppies in the world without adding more.

It is sometimes said that entire male dogs will do absolutely anything to get to a bitch in season, but this is very much down to the individual. In most pet dogs, an entire male dog need not be a problem to anyone. A bitch will bleed for around three weeks when she is in season – usually twice a year – and she will be more at risk from problems such as pyometra, a serious infection of the womb, if not spayed. On the other hand, a spayed bitch is more prone to become incontinent and the coat quality often changes in neutered dogs and bitches. Read up on all the facts, speak to your dog's breeder and your vet and make the best decision based on your, and your dog's, individual circumstances.

Walkies

Naturally, dogs need exercise every day. For young puppies, this should not entail long walks, as their growing bones could get damaged by over-use. This is especially true of large breeds. Take your puppy out and about, once it has been fully vaccinated, to get it used to the world. But allow it to toddle around at its own pace in the park. Proper walks need to wait until your dog is at the very least six months old. Do not make the mistake though of not taking your puppy out at all, as socialisation at a young age is vital. If your puppy is kept at home until several months old, it may be terrified on first seeing a car, a person riding a bike or even other dogs.

Take your puppy out and about, once it has been fully vaccinated

Grooming

All dogs need regular grooming. Find out your breed's requirements for specific instructions – your dog's breeder will be able to advise you, as will any dog groomer. Very short-

DOGS

haired dogs like boxers will only need a quick session with a rubber brush a couple of times a week – more often when they are shedding. Medium-coated short-haired dogs such as labradors and wire-coated breeds like many terriers will need brushing with a slicker brush a few times a week.

A slightly long coat such as that of a border collie or golden retriever will need brushing and combing several times a week. Very long-coated breeds, such as yorkshire terriers and shih-tzus, will need daily combing. When grooming your dog, also check ears, teeth and eyes to make sure they are all clean and check the body for fleas, sores or lumps. Your vet will supply you with the most effective flea treatments, ensuring your dog need never catch fleas.

Your dog's claws may need clipping every few weeks, although this depends largely on what surface your dog is exercised on. A dog that always runs on grass will have claws that grow long quicker than one that regularly exercises on a hard surface where they are worn down.

Regular baths are a must for most dogs, especially if the weather is wet and your dog has become muddy. Even so, these must not be too frequent. For most dogs, a bath every other month is sufficient. If bathed too often the natural oils present in the dog's coat will be destroyed and this can cause problems. If your dog gets very dirty when out for a walk, shower it off without using shampoo. All dogs will have a 'doggy' smell; this is natural and should not mean they need bathing every week.

All dogs need to be trained. It doesn't matter if you have a chihuahua or a Great Dane

Training

ALL dogs need to be trained. It doesn't matter if you have a chihuahua or a Great Dane, every single dog needs basic training. A well-behaved dog is much easier to live with and will also be a much happier dog. It is in a dog's nature to follow the pack leader and, to our pet dogs, the pack leaders are not other dogs but us, the humans in the family. Every dog needs to know its place in the pack and this will make it feel happy and

41

DOGS

secure. It is not at all cruel to train your dog, as long as it is done in a kind way. Most dogs love training. If there is a dog training club in your town, do sign up for classes. You will learn a lot and your dog will learn much better in a class environment than alone at home – it's important that all dogs behave when around other dogs and people.

Start training your dog within days of it arriving in your home. Do not make the mistake of waiting until you have already encountered problems, such as your dog not coming back when you call it, as it is much easier to prevent problems than solving them. Puppies learn very easily.

Always be kind to your dog. Do not shout at it, and never, ever hit it. Encourage good behaviour rather than punish bad. Use a 'half check' collar for puppies from about five months old and upwards – this is a collar that is part fabric or leather and part chain, and which tightens slightly when pulled. Younger puppies should just have a soft fabric or leather collar. Do not use choke chains. Choke chains are outdated and not needed in today's society where dogs are trained with kindness and encouragement, rather than force and punishment. A choke chain can seriously damage your dog's neck and throat.

For a lead, use a soft fabric lead or a leather lead, one that is pleasant to hold. Extending leads can be useful when training recalls, but are of little use in normal training as they are clumsy to hold and control.

Use treats if your dog is food motivated or just praise, to encourage your dog.

WHY DOES MY DOG DO THAT?

Lick my face?
Dogs greet other dogs they are friendly with by licking their faces. Puppies lick their mother's lips when hungry.

Drag his bottom on the ground?
This is a sign of your dog having impacted anal glands – see your vet. It is not usually a sign of worms.

Run away when I try to catch him?
Dogs love being chased. If your dog won't come when called, run away from him instead, to encourage him to come to you.

Mount other dogs, even of the same sex?
This is a sign of dominance.

Bark and chew when left alone?
Your dog may be suffering from separation anxiety and needs to gradually learn to be left on its own. Ask a dog trainer or behaviourist for help.

DOGS

Being clean in the house
House training should start as soon as your puppy arrives. Young puppies have small bladders and are not physically able to control their urination until they are older. Start house training on day one, but do not expect your puppy to be clean in the house until at least four months old, often older. In particular, expect accidents at night. Make cleaning easier by keeping your puppy confined to one room only, such as the kitchen. Every time your puppy has eaten, woken up after a nap or has had a play session, take it outside into the garden and wait until it goes. These are the times when most puppies will want to do their business. Praise your puppy when it performs. Do not scold it if it has an accident indoors, as this will not teach it anything, other than that you are unpleasant and do not like it doing its business – chances are next time your puppy will try to hide instead. Just clean the mess up and be more vigilant next time. When out for walks, always carry a plastic bag to pick up after your dog.

Coming when called
It is astounding how many dogs do not come back when their owners call them; in fact it is very easy to teach a puppy to come always when called. If you start with a young pup, you need never experience a problem and your dog can be given a lot of freedom with walks off the lead in parks, woods etc. Teach your puppy its name. Use your puppy's name a lot and always in nice ways. Call the puppy by name to give a treat or a cuddle and when feeding. It will learn its name in a day or so. When out for the first short walks, let your puppy off the lead in a secure area. Young puppies will follow their owners like little ducklings and do not want to be left alone. Make a habit of changing the direction you walk in without telling your puppy. Hide behind a bush, run away from your pup, calling its name. In no time at all, your pup will learn to keep its eyes on you and always follow you. Never wait for your puppy or run after it. It should keep his eyes on you, not the other way around. Call it frequently during walks just to praise it and release it again. Keep this up during all its life.

Training your dog to come when called is easy when you know how

DOGS

If your dog is an adult that is already in the habit of not coming when called, acquire an extendable lead or a long line and use this for training recalls. Call the dog and if it does not come, tug at the lead and haul it in as you run backwards, then praise your dog before letting it go again. Repeat this over and over again until it learns to come when called.

Sitting on command

The command 'sit' is one that will have many uses and one that all dogs can learn easily and quickly. Simply tell your dog 'sit' and gently push its backside into the sitting position. If you show the dog a treat and hold it above its head it will sit automatically. As soon as it sits, praise it and possibly give it a treat. Be consistent. Only say 'sit' once and if your dog does not sit immediately, gently make it sit. Do not repeat the command as that will only teach the dog that it does not have to listen. Only use one word as a command; don't say 'sit down' as this will confuse the dog. 'Sit' should mean one thing and 'down' quite another: your dog cannot do both at the same time.

Lying down on command

While holding a treat, show it to your dog. Place your hand on the floor with the treat in it, where the dog is sitting, and move it forwards. Gently place your other hand on the dog's shoulders and press slightly: your dog will most likely naturally drop into the down position. Give the command 'down' while the dog is going down. Praise it once it is down. Again, one word only: 'down', not 'lie down'. Some dominant dogs are not happy to lie down as it will put them in a submissive position to you, but with these you do need to persevere and, if necessary, firmly but gently push the dog into the down position. Praise the dog when it is down and relaxed, then say 'okay' as a release word indicating that the dog can now get up again. As long as you are consistent and use lots of praise, the dog will soon learn to drop down when told 'down', although it does usually take longer to master than the 'sit' command.

Staying

The 'stay' command is one of the most useful ones you could ever teach your dog. Imagine that you are walking your dog on

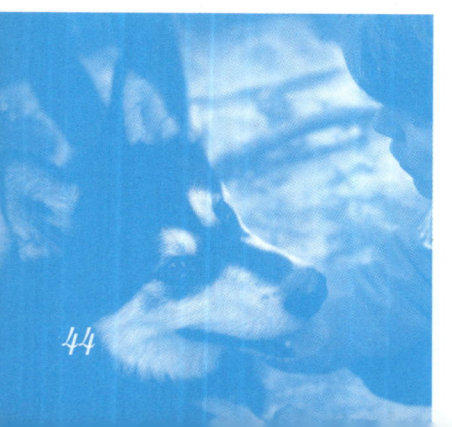

The command 'sit' is one that will have many uses and one that all dogs can learn easily and quickly

DOGS

the lead and you need to bend down to pick up its mess, if you are then able to tell it to sit and stay this will be easy – if it keeps moving around, it is not so easy! Not to mention that should your dog ever run towards a road or any other danger, a well-trained stay command may just save the dog's life!

You can teach the 'stay' in either a sit position, a down or even a stand, but it is easiest to start with a 'sit stay'. Tell your dog to sit and then tell it 'stay'. Show the dog the flat of your hand as a visual stay signal. The dog should be on a lead to start with. Take one step away from the dog and then quickly step back. If the dog does not move, praise it a lot. If it moves, put it back in the spot it was in and try again – you may need to tighten the lead upwards to stop the dog from coming towards you. The trick is to move away only a very short distance to start with and to return quickly, with lots of praise. Do not say, for example, 'Rufus, stay', as the dog will associate its name with being called and so will most likely NOT stay.

Make sure your dog walks well on a slack lead

Once your dog has understood what the stay command means, you can start staying away for slightly longer periods of time and then taking two steps instead of one, and then more and more, and dropping the lead onto the floor. As long as you do not rush the exercise and allow your dog to learn slowly over a period of time (usually a few weeks) all dogs can be taught a reliable stay – in fact it is perfectly possible to teach your dog to stay in one place even while you move out of sight.

Walking on the lead

It may sound obvious that all dogs should be able to walk on the lead, but if you look around yourself when out with your dog, you will no doubt spot a lot of dog owners who are being pulled around by their dogs, hardly even able to hold on to them. Walking a dog that pulls hard on the lead is not a pleasant experience at all so you need to make sure it walks well on a slack lead. Again, it is far easier to start with a young pup that has not developed bad habits.

With a very young pup, you will need first to get it used to wearing a collar and lead. Use a soft fabric collar and lightweight lead. The first time you put it on the pup, it will scratch at the

DOGS

collar and try to get it off. Distract your puppy by playing with it and it will soon forget it is wearing a collar. Don't forget to add an engraved metal disc with your name, address and telephone number to your dog's collar, as this is a legal requirement. It is also a very good idea to have your dog microchipped, as it can then always be traced to its owner if lost, even if it has lost its collar. The microchip contains a number that can be read by a special scanner and the number will match up to the dog's owner on a national database.

When you attach the lead to the collar, at first your puppy will most likely not want to walk at all. He or she may buck and try to walk backwards. Kneel down and call it, encouragingly. It's a good idea to practise lead walking in your back garden or even in the house before you venture out for an actual walk. With praise and encouragement your puppy will soon learn to follow you. This is when you need to make sure that it does not pull on the lead. Bad habits can form quickly and so you will want your puppy to walk on your left side, not dashing backwards and forwards in front of you, possibly tripping you up. A small puppy is unlikely to cause you a lot of problems if it pulls on the lead, but the same puppy may be difficult to hold if it still does the same when it is six months old! When the puppy pulls ahead, give a tug on the lead and say 'heel' and bring the puppy back to your side. Praise it when it is in the correct position at the side of you. Aim to have a slack lead and don't keep it too short – a short, tight lead will actually encourage the dog to pull. Again, be consistent and never allow the puppy to pull ahead.

For an older dog that has already learnt to pull, there are various ways of stopping this habit. One way is to simply stop walking as soon as the dog pulls, so that eventually it learns that it will get nowhere if it pulls. You can also change directions every time it starts to pull ahead. A head collar (there are several different brands available) can be extremely useful for an adult dog that pulls hard on the lead. The head collar will enable you to control the dog with ease and stop it pulling. When first used, your dog will not like it and will try to remove it, but with praise and encouragement he will get used to wearing the head collar. Compare how humans can control

One way to prevent a dog that has already learnt to pull on its lead is to simply stop every time it does so

DOGS

large horses with head collars – it is the same technique that we use with dogs.

Not jumping up

Few things can be so annoying as a dog that jumps up on people, especially if it has muddy paws. It's cute when a little puppy with dry paws does it, not so cute when a fully-grown labrador jumps up, almost knocks you over and ruins your clothes. Never allow the puppy to jump up on you, push it off gently and say a firm 'no'. Get down to the puppy's level instead. With adult dogs, turn your back to a dog that jumps up on you and ignore it. Give it praise and attention once it sits, and the dog will soon learn that it is far more rewarding not to jump.

Your dog may love being groomed before taking it to a show

Showing

Showing dogs can be a fun hobby for all ages. You can show your dog in conformation, where it is judged on its looks, or you can show it in obedience or agility, where it is your training and control over the dog that matters.

Most dog shows are conformation shows. Each breed has a written breed standard, which describes the way a dog of that particular breed should look. Breed standards are usually very specific when it comes to the dog's size, weight, colour, coat, body shape etc.

Always consult the breeder as to your dog's potential as a show dog

Not all purebred dogs are suitable for showing. Even if your dog seems like the most handsome dog in the world to you, it could still have some beauty fault that means it would always get overlooked in the show ring. Always consult your dog's breeder as to your dog's potential as a show dog. You will also need to find out from your breeder if your breed needs any special coat preparation or grooming for showing, as many do.

To be able to take part in most Kennel Club licensed shows, your dog must be registered with the Kennel Club in your name. If your dog is purebred but has no papers, you can still show it at companion shows. Companion shows are fun shows,

DOGS

> *If your dog is purebred but has no papers, you can still show it at companion shows*

held to raise money for good causes and here all dogs over six months old are welcome – with the exception of top show winners such as champions! No papers are needed. There will be breed classes, but not one for each breed, rather one per group of dogs, such as one for all sporting breeds (terriers, gundogs etc) and one for all non-sporting breeds (toy dogs, working and pastoral breeds etc). Then there are classes just for fun as well, along the lines of 'dog with the waggiest tail', 'best crossbreed' or 'dog most like its owner'. These shows are normally held outdoors in the summer and they are great fun for dog and owner alike, and a great place to start your dog's show career. Entries are made on the day and entry fees are minimal.

For more formal shows, both you and your dog will need to learn show handling. All show dogs must be able to stand still to be assessed by the judge and to run nicely around the ring. This is not as easy as it may seem, and can take a lot of practice. Different breeds are also handled in different ways. Ask your dog's breeder for advice and try to find a local dog training club or canine society that has ringcraft classes, as this is where you will learn to handle your dog at shows. You can then start showing at open shows, which are organised by various canine societies, and may include all breeds, a breed group or just one single breed. Entry must be made several weeks in advance. There are also limit shows, although these are quite rare. Entry to these is limited to dogs that have not won certain awards. The next level up is championship shows. Here you will find shows that may go on for two, three or even four days and again these may be for all breeds, certain breeds or just one. Often they are held at large venues such as racecourses and public parks, the dogs have to be benched when not in the judging ring rather than walked around all day and entry is large, with the popular breeds often having entries of many hundreds of dogs.

You can show your dog in conformation, where it is judged on its looks

DOGS

Breeding

The breeding of dogs is not something that should be undertaken lightly – and when done responsibly will cost you lots of money and take a lot of hard work. We have already discussed why it is best to buy your puppy from a responsible breeder and it will be obvious why you should only breed from healthy dogs that have had all their relevant health tests done, are of sound temperament, and preferably with good show results to ensure that they are good examples of their breed.

It will, needless to say, cost you a lot of money to have your bitch hip scored, eye tested, as well as a stud fee quite possibly (or, if you have a male dog as well, twice the fees for health testing). You may have to pay vet's fees if anything goes wrong and a caesarean can cost a lot of money. Rearing a litter of pups is expensive, as is having them registered. It will all cost a small fortune, so do not fall into the trap of believing that you will make a lot of money from breeding a litter – remember that is only likely to happen if you cut corners and do it the irresponsible way, possibly producing unhealthy puppies.

If you are determined to breed from your bitch and she is healthy, with all tests done, of good temperament and conforming well to her breed standard, then next you should consider whether you have the facilities for a litter of pups. You may well cope with a litter of yorkshire terrier puppies indoors, but a litter of labradors aged four weeks cannot stay in your house all the time as the mess will be indescribable! You will need a good outside kennel and run – more expense.

Also consider whether you can sell the puppies to good homes. Popular breeds such as golden retrievers and German shepherds and many others will have a lot of competition and, if you as a new breeder have a litter, you may find it hard to sell because many buyers will approach the more well-known, established breeders. What do you do if you find yourself with 10 puppies you are unable to sell? They are not much of a problem aged one week, but aged eight weeks, 10 puppies mean an awful lot of feeding and even more mess. There is also the question of

The breeding of dogs is not something that should be undertaken lightly

DOGS

time – you cannot possibly go to work when you have a litter of puppies.

Do consider breeding very carefully. Always consult the breeder of your bitch for advice and only go ahead if you are absolutely certain that you are doing the right thing.

Your new dog, whichever type you wish to own, is a huge commitment but once taken on it will become a companion for life.

GROOMING HINTS AND TIPS

- Find out your breed's requirements – many need professional trimming regularly
- Very short-coated dogs, like boxers, need grooming with a rubber-bristled brush once a week
- Short-coated breeds, like labradors, and wire-coated breeds, like westies, need grooming twice a week with a slicker brush and metal comb
- Long-coated breeds, like border collies, need grooming with a slicker brush and metal comb twice a week
- Very long-coated breeds, like rough collies, need grooming with a comb and brush daily
- Specks of black dirt in your dog's coat will indicate fleas – get treatment from your vet
- Get your dog used to being groomed regularly as a young pup – it will help your dog become used to being handled and examined and teaches it that you are in charge
- Don't bath your dog too frequently – if your dog has had a muddy walk, just rinse the coat with water. Bath every other month using a special dog shampoo – never one sold for human use

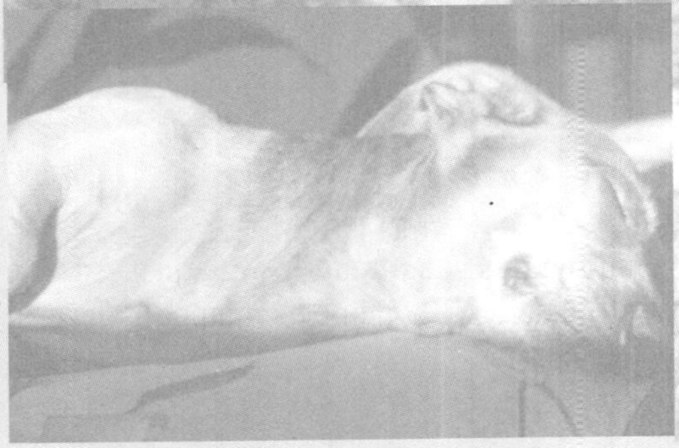

DOGS

RABBITS

Long before it became a much loved pet, the rabbit, being a robust and adaptable animal, successfully 'shadowed' humans for centuries, following them to most places on the planet. Wherever humans have settled and grown crops, the rabbit has not been far behind.

History of rabbits

The European rabbit, *Oryctolagus cuniculus*, is related to the large rodent family, but is classified within its own order, *Lagomorpha*, along with hares.

The ancient Romans recognised the worth of rabbits after they were imported into Italy *circa* 100BC. The Romans found that rabbits were an excellent source of cheap meat throughout their expanding empire.

It is documented that the Normans brought several hundred rabbits to England with them after their successful conquest in 1066 and this led to them spreading across the whole of the UK. In subsequent centuries, rabbits were introduced to the US and Australia – and in many areas they became a real pest by destroying crops.

The first rabbits kept as pets were in the early years of the 19th century, the time when many animal fancies sprang up. In the 1830s and 1840s, various rabbit enthusiasts – many of them farmers – began to develop new breeds of rabbit out of captive food stock.

One of the first domesticated rabbit breeds was the English lop, a large breed noticeable for its enormous ears. From here, many other new colours and coat types were developed and the concept of exhibiting these specimens in competition, rather like prize farm animals, came to the fore. Thus it was that many rabbit clubs sprang up, later leading to the organised rabbit fancy and later to rabbits becoming popular as children's pets.

RABBITS

Housing

The commonest form of rabbit house is a hutch. If the hutch is to be situated outside, it must be well waterproofed and able to withstand the elements. The hutch should be made of wood, as plastic or metal will become far too cold in winter or too hot in summer.

The very best type of hutch is made of heavy wood in tongue-and-groove style. The extra expenditure on a sturdy hutch will save money and serve your rabbit better, in the long term.

The most suitable type of hutch will have a separate sleeping compartment or a partially covered front. This is important so that your rabbit can take shelter during bad weather. Usually, one third of the hutch front will be covered by wood, the remainder being made from tough metal wire.

The very best type of hutch is made of heavy wood in tongue-and-groove style

The ideal roof will either be an apex, or be sloped, preferably with a slight overhang over the front of the hutch to allow rainwater to drip away without going inside the hutch. The roof should be covered with sturdy roofing felt.

The hutch should never be placed directly on the ground; it should always be raised by at least 5cm (2in). This will make the hutch warmer and drier for its occupant and will prevent the base from rotting. Some hutches come complete with short legs, although you can raise the hutch yourself by placing it on top of some bricks or paving slabs.

Most breeds of rabbit will benefit from having an outside run, particularly during the summer months

The actual siting of the hutch is also important. It should not be placed somewhere fully exposed to the elements. The ideal place is with its back against the wall of the house or outbuilding to provide maximum protection against bad weather.

The floor should be covered with good quality wood shavings available from any pet store. Hutches should also have a layer or straw placed over the wood shavings in the winter months for added protection from rain, as even the best protected hutches can become very damp if rain drives in and soaks the shavings.

RABBITS

Bedding is quite simple: clean, fresh, meadow hay is by far the best bedding, keeping the rabbit warm and snug. The rabbit will also eat the hay, providing essential roughage in its diet.

Outside runs

Most breeds of rabbit will benefit from having an outside run, particularly during the summer months – and it is all good exercise.

A good run is usually made of wood and wire, big enough for rabbits to move about freely, with a lid for safety. The run is placed on the lawn, letting blades of grass grow through the wire base, allowing the rabbit to nibble the grass. Ideally, the run should have a small, enclosed area to enable the rabbit to take shelter from rain or hot sun.

Hay is essential in a rabbit's diet, as well as being useful as bedding

Feeding

Nowadays, there are a huge range of rabbit feeds on the market and it can be quite a headache for the new owner to select one. There are, and always will be, proprietary rabbit pellets, which are said to provide all of a rabbit's dietary needs, but most rabbit foods are complete mixes of corn, oats and biscuit meal.

A good quality rabbit mix will contain oats, barley, flakes of dried peas and maize, biscuit meal and a few pellets. This is enough for even the fussiest eater to find something they like.

It is best to place your rabbit's food in a solid, earthenware bowl, which is heavy enough to prevent the rabbit from tipping it over. That said, if a rabbit is determined to upend a food bowl, it will do so, irrespective of the weight!

As mentioned above, hay is essential to provide the rabbit with roughage in its diet, as well as being useful as bedding, so a quantity of hay should always be available.

Rabbits do enjoy vegetables and fruit, although these should never be fed in large quantities, as they can easily upset their stomachs and cause diarrhoea. 'Hard' greens such as carrots,

ACCESSORIES

- Toys
- A sturdy wooden rabbit hutch, preferably with a felted roof
- Strong earthenware or metal food bowls
- Water bottle
- Small brush and comb for grooming
- Clippers for claws

RABBITS

turnips, cabbage and apple are relished as a supplement to the regular diet.

Clean drinking water should always be available, as rabbits drink a lot. The best method of providing the water is via a gravity water bottle attached to the rabbit's cage or hutch.

Rabbits may be observed eating their droppings, which can look rather disconcerting. This is nothing to worry about and is perfectly natural, as rabbits practise refection in the wild. It is simply a way of extracting the maximum protein and goodness from their food – a sort of 'extra digestion'.

Acquiring a rabbit

Your local pet shop is a good starting point for purchasing a rabbit. Most pet shops buy in either crossbred rabbits or those of specific breeds that are excess to a fancier's requirements. Alternatively, contact a local rabbit club for details of rabbit breeders in your area.

If you are after a specific breed of rabbit, you will be spoilt for choice! There are over 100 different breeds of rabbit in existence today. Some of these will make excellent pets; others are far more specialised and suitable only for the experienced rabbit keepers. Good pets can be made from the English and Dutch breeds. The small Netherland dwarf, the dwarf and mini lops are the best pets in the lop family.

Small breeds such as the Polish are flighty and can sometimes be quite bad-tempered, while giant breeds such as the French lop and chinchilla giganta need a lot of space and attention, and really are best kept by the serious rabbit keeper.

Truly exotic varieties, such as the Angora, with its long, silky coat and, to a certain extent, the Cashmere lop, which also has long fur, are more specialist in their requirements and are the province of the serious fancier.

There are over 100 different breeds of rabbit in existence today

RABBITS

General care and maintenance

Rabbits are generally very hardy animals, especially if kept outdoors in suitable conditions, but the old adage of 'prevention is better than cure' is a sound one. Obviously, there are certain viruses that can affect rabbits and will attack any rabbit, no matter how well looked after, so an owner must always be vigilant as to the rabbit's general well being.

Remember to give them plenty of attention, as boredom can affect rabbits badly. There are plenty of amusing rabbit toys available in pet shops nowadays. Even something as simple as a small ball or even a small, hard, plastic or wood dumbbell toy, as used by small dogs, can provide a rabbit with amusement.

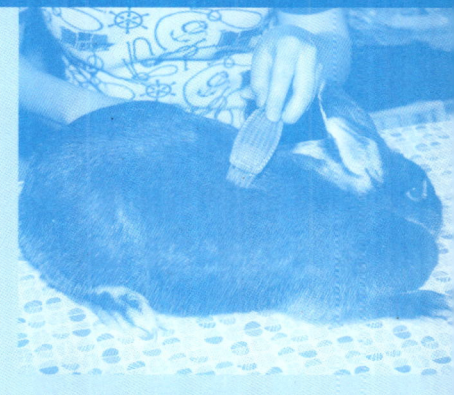

Even if you don't have a long-haired rabbit, it is a good idea to buy a small brush or comb to groom your rabbit now and again

It will be necessary to clip the rabbit's claws on a regular basis. Most owners can learn to carry out this procedure with a bit of practice. It is usually best to sit down and lay the rabbit on its back on your lap, while you trim the claws. The rabbit's coat needs to be kept clean and well groomed.

Rabbits' teeth can become overgrown, sometimes caused by a lack of items to gnaw or by a hereditary disease called malocclusion. This will necessitate regular trips to the vet to have their teeth trimmed, although, with a strong pair of clippers and some practice, it is entirely possible to learn to clip them yourself, following the same procedure for clipping a rabbit's claws.

Although rabbits are very hardy animals and can survive quite cold conditions, they cannot survive very wet conditions for long, so their hutches and cages should always be kept clean and dry, being cleaned out once a week at least.

Even if you don't have a long-haired rabbit, it is a good idea to buy a small brush or comb to groom your rabbit now and again, to help keep its coat clean and free from dirt or pieces of hay.

Properly cared for, a rabbit will live for an average of five years. Smaller breeds tend to be longer lived than large breeds and, in some cases, have been known to make it to as old as 10!

RABBITS

Breeding

The female rabbit (doe) can be mated for the first time at the age of around five to six months. Do not attempt to mate a doe earlier, as an immature doe will not look after her litter properly. Large breeds, such as the French lop, take longer to mature, so, with a doe of a very large breed, it is best to wait until she is nine months.

It is equally important that the doe is not too old to be used for breeding. In the case of a doe that has not previously had any litters, she must not be older than 12 months when her first litter is born. Before this age her pelvis will be soft and can stretch when she gives birth. After 12 months, the pelvis bone will have fused into position and, unless previously stretched, will not open properly to allow the doe to give birth.

The male rabbit (buck), who doesn't have to endure the strain of being pregnant and raising a litter, can often be used for breeding from the age of four or five months and will continue being sexually active up until the age of five years.

The first rule of mating rabbits is that it should never, ever be done in the doe's hutch. The doe will defend her hutch or cage from intruders and will no doubt attack any passing buck. The mating should, therefore, take place in either the buck's quarters or on neutral ground.

The female rabbit is one of the few animals that can be mated even when she is not on heat. The actual act of mating will trigger the doe to ovulate, so a mating done at any time stands a good chance of being successful.

Assuming that your doe is in heat and willing to be mated, place her in the buck's quarters or the designated mating cage. Hopefully, mating will take place immediately. Most breeds need careful supervision, in case of fights developing after mating, although, in placid breeds such as the Netherland dwarf, the pair can usually be left together overnight.

The gestation period for a rabbit is 28-34 days, with 30-32 days being the average. It can be quite difficult to tell if a doe is pregnant or not, as, unlike other gravid (pregnant) rodents, the vast majority of rabbits do not look pregnant.

RABBITS

The first clear sign that the doe is pregnant is when you see her preparing a nest for the forthcoming litter. She will usually construct the nest in a corner of the hutch or cage and it will consist of hay and/or straw, lined with fur that the doe will pluck from her own abdomen. The nest is very important; any babies born or kept outside of a warm nest will not survive for long, as they will be too cold.

Around 27 days after the mating, her hutch should be cleaned out and filled with plenty of wood shavings and/or straw, with a good supply of fresh hay. It is vital that the doe has plenty of nesting material. Make sure, too, that food and water are available at all times, as a thirsty or hungry doe may occasionally kill and eat her babies after the birth.

Most rabbits give birth during the night or early hours of the morning when it is quiet and no one is around. It is very rare to see any signs of the birth, such as blood: the hutch or cage will look perfectly clean. The only way to see if the doe has given birth is to inspect the nest. Keep a close eye on the doe or remove her from the hutch, as she may attack any intruder after the litter has been born.

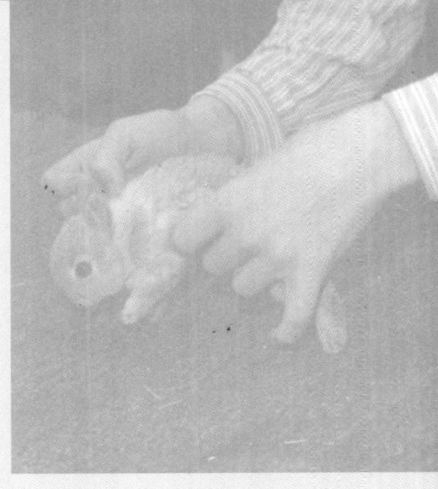

This demonstrates the correct way to to lift a baby rabbit

Make sure that food and water are available at all times – a thirsty or hungry doe may occasionally kill and eat her babies

A normal litter size for a small breed, such as a Polish or Netherland dwarf, can range between one and six, with two to four being the average. Does of small breeds can usually cope with up to six babies. Slightly larger breeds, such as the dwarf lop, will usually have litters consisting of three to five babies, although nine is not unheard of. Giant breeds have very large litters, with anything from five to twelve kits being quite common.

Rabbit kits are born naked, but they have a hint of pigmentation at birth, which allows you to distinguish between pale and dark coloured animals immediately after the birth, although they rapidly grow fur after this. The kits will start to leave the nest once their eyes have opened, usually between 10 to 14 days of age. They will now start to explore their surroundings and you should start to handle them regularly – and carefully – to get

RABBITS

them used to human beings. Once the kits have left the nest, the whole family will need a very large supply of food. The kits will be able to eat the same food as their mother, as their teeth will have developed. Make sure that you use a food bowl that the babies can easily reach into.

As to how long the babies stay with their mother depends solely on the mother. Most does will let their babies know in no uncertain terms when they have had enough of them. The doe will chase the kits and nip them if they come too close. Usually, most breeds will tolerate their offspring for five or six weeks, which is the ideal weaning age.

Showing

As with most pets, rabbits are very popular show animals and there are many rabbit clubs to be found, some regional, some specialist, some national, with the result that you could probably go to a rabbit show every weekend of the year if you wanted to!

Competition can be quite intense at some rabbit shows

Most rabbit clubs are affiliated to a main governing body, so it is best to get in touch with this first and enquire about joining and also registering your rabbits with them if need be.

Competition is quite intense at some shows, although at most ordinary, small club shows it's quite good-natured and fun. Of course, going to a show brings you into contact with other rabbit lovers, so that's a good thing in itself.

Sussex gold and cream rabbits

Health (see Houserabbits)

HOUSERABBITS

Who'd have thought that rabbits, traditionally outdoor pets, would be sharing our homes as possible replacement pets to dogs and cats? But this is the beauty of houserabbits who are now occupying a space in their owners' homes as well as their affections.

Rabbits come in from the cold

In the past couple of decades, pet rabbits have been seen in a completely different light. They continue to be among the most popular pets, ranking in fourth place behind cats, dogs and fish in the UK, the US and Australia. But they are now increasingly seen as house pets, a perfectly acceptable alternative to dogs and cats, and the ideal pet for the busy, career-minded family or individual.

It all started back in America during the yuppie days of the late 1980s, when busy young executives craved the company of a pet when they eventually returned home after a hard day at the office. They needed a pet that didn't need to be taken for walks, didn't require too much one-to-one contact and one that could amuse itself while they were away. Houserabbits fitted the bill perfectly.

As it happens, there's nothing all that unusual about houserabbits in other parts of the world. In countries such as Sweden it is the norm to keep rabbits indoors, as the cold climate is not conducive to keeping them in outdoor hutches.

The craze for houserabbits crossed the Atlantic in the mid-1990s and caught on in the UK in a big way. Nowadays, the British Houserabbit Association records a membership of over 2,000 houserabbit aficionados — over twice the number of 'serious' rabbit fanciers.

Rabbits are increasingly seen as house pets, a perfectly acceptable alternative to dogs and cats

HOUSERABBITS

Acquiring a houserabbit

Rabbits can, of course, be purchased from pet shops, although they may not necessarily be marketed specifically as houserabbits. Alternatively, they can be purchased from a breeder. A houserabbit club can give you information on suitable breeders and places to purchase a houserabbit of your own, so it's always a good idea to check with them first.

If you asked half a dozen houserabbit owners which is the best breed of rabbit to keep as a houserabbit, you'd get half a dozen different answers. Perhaps, for the average family, small and medium sized breeds such as dwarf lop and mini lop, Dutch or English would be best. These are quite affable rabbits, which are not only affectionate towards humans, but also quite ready to mix with other pet animals. The author's own mini lop houserabbit used to play daily with several of his cats, as well as golden retrievers! All that was required was a careful, supervised introduction (after all, some breeds of dogs or cats just don't take to other animals) and a close eye on proceedings for the first few times that the two parties met.

Housing

British giant and Netherland dwarf rabbits, the latter being a popular choice

There are many indoor rabbit cages available on the market. These range in size and price, but the essential features of any such cage are that it should have a sturdy, plastic bottom tray and a strong, well-fitted, wire canopy to keep the rabbit in and other pets out. Once the cage has been purchased, it needs to be furnished. To start with, the floor should be covered with good quality wood shavings – again, available from any pet store. Shavings are preferable to sawdust, as rabbits can inhale the dust, causing them to sneeze. It may even cause nasal infections and breathing difficulties, or can damage their eyes. A layer of straw will keep the shavings in place and also help keep the cage dry.

The size of the cage is very important. The simple rule of thumb is the bigger the rabbit, the bigger the hutch or cage. As a general guideline, a home for one small breed of rabbit, such

HOUSERABBITS

as a Netherland dwarf, should be no less than 90cm x 60cm (36in x 24in). For a larger breed such as a Dutch or New Zealand, the home should be no less than 120cm x 60cm (48in x 24in). The giant breeds, such as French lops, need significantly larger cages.

Ideally the cage should have a hayrack fitted to the side and come complete with a water bottle. Such cages are relatively easy to clean out and, crucially, kept free of odour!

The indoor cage should be sited at a location to suit both owner and rabbit. If the rabbit is to be 'free range', coming and going as it pleases, then the cage should be placed in a suitable location in a chosen room – a corner area being ideal.

Even the cleanest, best house-trained rabbit can make a mess and kick shavings out of its cage, so the cage should be placed on a plastic sheet, or newspaper, which extends beyond the cage, in order to catch any debris.

Houserabbits should be fed the same sort of diet as ordinary pet rabbits

Feeding

Houserabbits should be fed just like ordinary pet rabbits, mainly with a good quality dry mix of corn, oats, pellets and crushed, dried vegetables, obtainable from any good pet shop. Hay is not only useful as bedding, but also forms a part of the rabbit's diet, providing necessary roughage.

Hay is not only useful as bedding, but also forms a part of the rabbit's diet, providing roughage

Vegetables and fruit are always welcome as they are for outdoor rabbits, although 'greens' should not be fed to excess, as this can cause the rabbit to suffer from diarrhoea – not a good thing around the house! Fresh drinking water should always be available, best provided in a gravity water bottle attached to the cage.

Care and maintenance

When you acquire your houserabbit, it will need a short time to adjust to life in your home. Leave the rabbit in its cage for a couple of days, still attending to its needs, talking to it and

HOUSERABBITS

ACCESSORIES CHECK LIST

- Toys
- A suitably sized cage, ideally complete with hayrack
- Earthenware food bowls
- Water bottle
- Litter tray
- Plastic tubing to encase electrical wiring around the house
- Harness and lead

If you want to take your houserabbit for a walk make sure it is wearing a special rabbit harness

stroking it to gain its trust. Giving it a few treats and titbits always helps to break the ice in any human-rabbit relationship.

After this, open the cage door and let the rabbit wander out, but be careful to supervise any naughty behaviour, such as chewing telephone cables and electrical wires which may not have been 'rabbit-proofed'! This can easily be done by encasing the wires in plastic tubing, which can be purchased from garden centres and hardware stores. Some computer shops sell special computer cable covers, made of thick plastic, which are ideal.

Walkies

Of course, your houserabbit can be taken outdoors, either to enjoy cropping the lawn in a special outdoor run or taken for walks. If you want to take your houserabbit for a walk, however, make sure it is wearing a special rabbit harness and that you have control of it on a lead. It's always advisable to practise going for a walk with the rabbit in your own garden, to allow the rabbit to get used to wearing the harness and so that it is not afraid to hop alongside you. As to where to walk your rabbit, on the grass in the local park is a good enough place, as long as you keep an eye out for dogs and other dangers. Walking down the high street is not the best place for any rabbit to be, so the best thing then is to carry it. Bear in mind though that rabbits are not dogs and they can easily get tired.

Litter training

If a houserabbit is to wander around your home, it is going to need somewhere to 'do its business', so a litter tray (or two or three) should be provided in suitable locations. These will need to be filled with soft peat, wood shavings or, ideally, cat litter, which isn't so easy for the rabbit to kick out of the tray. The best sort of cat litter would be the wood-based variety, which is both lightweight and more user friendly.

HOUSERABBITS

The rabbit can be trained to use its litter tray quite simply. The best approach is to take some droppings from the rabbit's cage and place these in the litter tray, thus indicating to the rabbit that this is a toilet area. Also, when the rabbit is seen to 'squat' on the floor, simply pick it up and place it in the litter tray. They learn remarkably fast and, although there may be the odd accident from time to time, the houserabbit will become housetrained quite quickly.

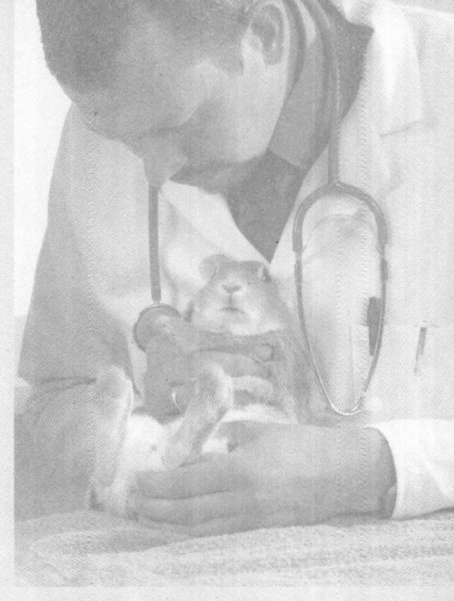

Your houserabbit will need to be vaccinated by your vet

HEALTH CARE

- Just as your cat needs to be vaccinated, your houserabbit will need to be vaccinated by your vet against the two killer diseases, myxomatosis and Rabbit Viral Haemorrhagic Disease (RVHD). Thereafter, it should receive annual booster injections.

- All rabbits' claws will need regular clipping once every six weeks. With a bit of practice it is quite possible for you, the owner, to carry this procedure out, using a pair of strong nail cutters, the same as those used to clip cats' claws.

- Rabbits do not need to be treated against fleas, as they do not carry them. However, if flea spraying your carpet, be careful that you don't accidentally spray the rabbit, as it may have a bad reaction to the spray.

- It is a good idea to have houserabbits neutered, as it reduces their territorial instincts and tones down any aggressive tendencies to defend a territory. After all, nobody wants to share their home with a pet that is going to defend its own patch!

GUINEA PIGS

Most people call them guinea pigs, fanciers call them cavies, the ancient Incas called them dinner. These robust little South American rodents were first domesticated over 1,000 years ago by the Incas and kept in pens next to their owners' homes to be eaten as required, providing a valuable source of protein for the whole family.

History of guinea pigs

When the Spanish conquistadors invaded and subjugated the Incas in the 16th century, they were very taken with the cavies, which they named cochinillo das Indas – literally 'Little Indian Pigs' – and began to export them to Europe as animals for meat. It is believed that the cavy later gained its popular name of guinea pig after being brought into Europe via the Spanish dominion of Spanish Guiana, which led to them being dubbed guiana pigs, later, guinea pigs.

In the UK, cavies became popular pets during the 19th century and were later much prized as exhibition animals, becoming almost as popular as fancy rabbits. Like rabbits, they were bred in a wide range of colours, markings and different coat types. In a short space of time, guinea pigs (as we shall call them) were exported around the world, becoming firm favourites in the US and Europe.

Today, the guinea pig remains a firm favourite both as a pet and an exhibition animal, although always slightly behind rabbits on both counts. It must be said that guinea pigs are not the most intelligent of rodents, but they are very vocal, emitting high-pitched squeaks, especially when hungry and expecting feeding time. They have a certain *joie de vivre* and barmy eccentricity all of their own, which makes them quite endearing as pets.

The Latin name for the guinea pig is *Cavia porcellus*, another reference to the animal's pig-like appearance. Although they are rodents, they belong to the sub-order *Hystriocomorpha*, a group that includes chinchillas and capybara. In this group the facial muscles and structure is far more developed than in 'mainstream' rodents. Guinea pigs

GUINEA PIGS

have the characteristic broad nasal passages and pronounced cheekbones of the animals in this order.

Guinea pigs do not vary hugely in body size, measuring about 20cm (8in) long and weighing roughly between 900g and 1200g (32-42oz), males (boars) being slightly larger than females (sows).

Housing

Guinea pigs may be kept as indoor or outdoor pets and to this end there is plenty of suitable housing available on the pet market. A sturdy wooden rabbit hutch makes an ideal outdoor home, while a plastic cage with a metal wire canopy is the best type of indoor home.

The minimum size for a cage or hutch for a single guinea pig should be no less than 45cm x 30cm x 30 cms (18in x 12in x 12in), although the larger, the better. Guinea pigs will live happily as a breeding pair and, unlike many other rodents, will not breed to excess. However, a single sex pair will obviously prevent unwanted offspring. Sows will happily co-exist together. Boars are best housed singly, as they have a tendency to fight.

If the guinea pig is to be housed outdoors, make sure that the hutch has a screened-off sleeping compartment, which will provide shelter from the weather. The hutch is also best raised off the ground by at least a few inches, to prevent dampness and also to deter predators, such as cats, dogs and foxes. The hutch should also be placed in a sheltered spot and out of direct sunlight in hot weather.

Fresh sawdust or wood shavings should be used as substrate on the hutch or cage floor, with a layer of straw on top to prevent the wood shavings from becoming too wet or soiled. Plenty of fresh hay should be provided, both as bedding and as a food supplement, providing necessary roughage in the guinea pig's diet.

During the summer months, guinea pigs will enjoy being placed in an outdoor run. This is a simple wooden and wire

ACCESSORIES CHECK LIST

- Good quality hutch or cage
- Strong earthenware or metal food bowl
- Gravity water bottle
- Grooming brush and comb for long-haired varieties

Guinea pigs may be kept as indoor or outdoor pets

GUINEA PIGS

construction, which can be made easily or purchased from a pet store. The run is placed on the lawn, allowing grass to protrude through the base. The guinea pig is then placed in the run and will eat the grass and enjoy the fresh air. The run should have an enclosed covered area to enable the guinea pig to shelter from strong sunlight or rain, and to avoid any danger from lurking neighbourhood predators.

In the UK, guinea pigs became popular pets during the 19th century and were later much prized as exhibition animals

Feeding

The standard diet for a guinea pig is quite simple, consisting of a basic dry mix of corn, crushed oats and dried peas. There are several proprietary brands of guinea pig mix available through pet shops, so providing the basic diet should never be a problem.

Green food is a vitally important part of the guinea pig's diet as the guinea pig is the only small animal that cannot manufacture its own vitamin C inside its body, so this must be derived from its food. This is a trait which guinea pigs share with human beings.

Carrots, celery, lettuce, broccoli, apples, pears, tomatoes, swede and cucumbers are all vegetables and fruits relished by guinea pigs. However, there is a lot to be said for wild greens, such as dandelion leaves, clover and grass, all of which are cheaply and readily available during the warmer months of the year. Never feed your guinea pig any such greens which have been cut with a lawnmower or they will be contaminated with oil. Also, always wash any hand-picked wild greens thoroughly to remove any lingering parasites or even insecticides that could prove harmful to your pet.

Guinea pigs have a certain joie de vivre and barmy eccentricity all of their own

Food is best placed in an earthenware bowl, which will be too heavy for the guinea pig to tip up, or a metal hopper attached to the cage or hutch bars. Fresh drinking water should always be available daily and is best provided via a gravity water bottle attached to the bars.

GUINEA PIGS

Acquiring a guinea pig

Guinea pigs are relatively easy to come by, being sold through most pet shops. However, if you want a 'pedigree' piggy that you could exhibit at shows, then visiting a breeder is your best bet.

Guinea pigs are available in a bewildering range of varieties. Colour types include red, cream, black, lilac, gold, albino, chocolate and many more. Marked varieties include dalmatian, Dutch (a two-tone variety, similar to the Dutch rabbit), Himalayan and tortoiseshell. The different coat types include satin, where the guinea pig may be of any standard colour or marking, with a glossy, shiny coat. Then there is the Abyssinian (with its fur dotted with small 'rosettes'), crested, Sheltie (with 'back-swept' long hair), curly-coated Rex, Peruvian (with an incredibly long coat which can reach a length of up to 6cm (2in), Texel (a curly coated Sheltie) and Alpaca (a curly-coated Peruvian).

Varieties such as the Peruvian and Sheltie need extra care by being groomed regularly. This should be carefully borne in mind when selecting the best type of guinea pig for you.

Of course, there are also numerous crossbred 'piggies' to be found in pet shops, while many breeders often advertise young guinea pigs for sale which do not quite make the show grade but which will be ideal as pets.

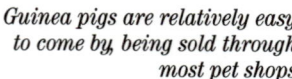
Guinea pigs are relatively easy to come by, being sold through most pet shops

Breeding

Guinea pigs are relatively easy to breed. As mentioned, a pair will not breed excessively and often take a break after two litters. Boars are sexually mature at three months old, while sows tend to reach sexual maturity at four months. The sow must be mated before she reaches about eight to ten months or else her pelvic bones will fuse and she might never be able to give birth.

The sow comes into oestrus every 14 to 16 days where she is receptive to the boar. Mating is usually quite obvious and often very noisy! Unlike other rodents, guinea pigs have a long

GUINEA PIGS

gestation period, between 63 and 72 days. After 50 days, the sow's condition is obvious and you can see the babies moving inside her abdomen. About four days before birth, the sow's pelvic bones will move apart slightly and she will soon be ready to deliver her offspring.

The litter usually numbers between two and three, although larger litters have been recorded. The sow makes no nest and usually gives birth during the night, so ensure that there is plenty of bedding available for the babies.

Unlike most other rodents, guinea pig babies are born fully developed, with fur, and their eye and ears open. They will suckle from their mother for four to five weeks, but will often begin to nibble on their parents' food within hours of being born, as their teeth are also fully developed.

They need no special diet, and may remain with their mother – and father – until the age of six weeks, by which time they are weaned and may be removed to their own cages.

They are easily sexed. Simply hold the guinea pig on its back (holding it firmly but gently). The boar's genitalia are in the shape of a circle, whilst the sow's are Y-shaped. Older boars have very obvious testicles and thus are very easy to sex.

This is how you should pick up your new guinea pig

Showing

Guinea pigs are very popular show animals and there are many local, regional and specialist cavy clubs to be found, most of which stage shows of different grades and level of importance at least once or twice a month. It is best to find a national cavy society via specialist magazines or the internet and make contact with them and they will put you in touch with your nearest club.

Guinea pigs will respond to gentle handling, although they feel far more secure on the floor than when being held

GUINEA PIGS

General care and maintenance

Guinea pigs are quite robust little animals and are generally longer-lived than their rodent relatives, with an average lifespan of four to five years.

They enjoy being let out of their hutches or cages for exercise, although they are happy running free in an outdoor run or a carefully sectioned off area indoors. They will respond well to gentle handling, although they feel far more secure on the floor than when being held. Guinea pigs can often squirm if held and a fall from any sort of height could prove fatal!

The hutch or cage should be cleaned out at least once a week and thoroughly washed and disinfected every two or three months. All uneaten fresh food should be removed after 24 hours otherwise it will go off and could turn mouldy or attract flies.

Guinea pigs are very popular show animals

GUINEA PIGS

COMMON AILMENTS

- Diarrhoea: This is usually caused by feeding the guinea pig too much vegetable matter. Simply cut out any greens (but ensure the guinea pig has plenty of water, dry food and hay) until the diarrhoea stops, then reintroduce a smaller amount of green food. Arrowroot biscuits in the dry mix can help relieve the symptoms of diarrhoea.

- Worms: Like cats and dogs, guinea pigs can sometimes suffer from worms, especially if they eat grass that has been contaminated by cats or other worm-carrying animals. The small, white worms can be seen easily in the guinea pig's droppings. Visit your vet, who will prescribe a suitable liquid wormer, usually one intended for kittens. Do not attempt to worm a guinea pig yourself without seeking veterinary advice beforehand.

- Lice and other parasites: Guinea pigs are prone to lice infestations, usually from hay or straw. The guinea pig may be sprayed with a suitable flea spray, or bathed in an insecticidal shampoo for cats or other small animals. The treatment usually takes place twice within 14 days. Seek advice from your vet or pet shop.

- Overgrown or broken teeth: Guinea pigs have 20 teeth, four large incisor teeth at the front (two at the top and two at the bottom) and 16 at the back of their mouths. If a guinea pig is not given enough hard food (such as carrots), the teeth may grow too long. In the case of the front teeth, this will be obvious to see. It can be more difficult to tell if the back teeth have overgrown. Over-long teeth will cause the guinea pig feeding problems and it will lose weight. Seek veterinary treatment to have the animal's teeth clipped and filed down.

RATS

A rat may seem an unlikely choice for a much-loved pet, but, in today's ever-changing world, a domestic pet with unsavoury connctations will raise a few eyebrows. After all, rats are associated with bubonic plague, horror movies and gruesome legends such as that of the Pied Piper of Hamelin. But domesticated rats – or fancy rats to give them their correct title – are clean, tame, easy to handle and highly intelligent. They will even learn to respond to their own names. They are widely available nowadays, thanks to their growing popularity as pets and show animals and are suitable as a pet for anyone aged six and upwards.

History of rats

There are two species of rat in the world, *Rattus rattus*, the black or ship rat, and *Rattus norvegicus*, the brown or Norway rat. Both originated in Asia, the black species is quite slender with a very long tail and sharp snout, while the brown species is larger, with a more compact body, and is generally hardier and more adaptable. Black rats were first spread around the world by early traders and invaders, such as the Phoenicians and later the Romans.

The black rat became widespread throughout Europe and gained notoriety by being the unwitting carrier of bubonic plague which wiped out millions of people – about one third of the population of Europe – in the Middle Ages. The plague itself was carried in the bodies of fleas carried by the rats and so transferred to human beings very easily.

The brown rat spread across the world in the early 18th century, reaching Britain in 1714. It acquired the name Norway rat, because it was erroneously supposed that the rat arrived on board timber ships coming to Britain from Norway. In fact, the rat did not reach Norway until at least 1762, reaching the Americas around the same time. The brown rat, being larger and hardier than its smaller relative, became the dominant species, displacing the black rats. Nowadays, the black rat is extremely rare in the UK and is confined to isolated colonies in rural areas.

RATS

It seems bizarre, but it was a rat catcher who first started the trend for pet rats. In fact, it was no less a person than Jack Black, Royal Ratcatcher to Queen Victoria, who extolled the virtues of domesticated rats. Black was, to say the least, a character, famed in Victorian London for his legendary rat-catching skills, often telling lurid tales of the worst and most vicious rats he ever came across, or the best terrier dogs that he bred.

Most of Black's live-caught rats were sold on to the infamous rat pits in pubs, where patrons would wager upon how many rats a terrier could dispatch in a set time. One of Black's best customers was Jemmy Shaw, who, like Black, was fascinated by a few odd coloured specimens among the various catches.

These they kept and bred together, producing the first pet rats, which they sold to well-off young ladies to keep as pets.

Some years later, fancy rats, now well established, were taken up for exhibition purposes, largely thanks to the efforts of one Miss Mary Douglas who championed the cause of fancy rats. The first-ever classes for fancy rats were staged at Aylesbury in 1901 and, through the National Mouse Club, fancy rats remained popular for close on three decades.

There were various rat 'revivals' during the 1950s and 1960s, but it was not until 1976 that the National Fancy Rat Society was founded in the UK by herpetologist Geoff Izzard and teacher Joan Pearce. The rat fancy spread to the US in 1978 and to many European countries including Sweden, Finland, Norway, France and Germany.

Nowadays, fancy rats are bred in a bewildering range of varieties and have become accepted as great pets for young and old alike.

It was a rat catcher who first started the trend for pet rats – Jack Black, Royal Ratcatcher to Queen Victoria

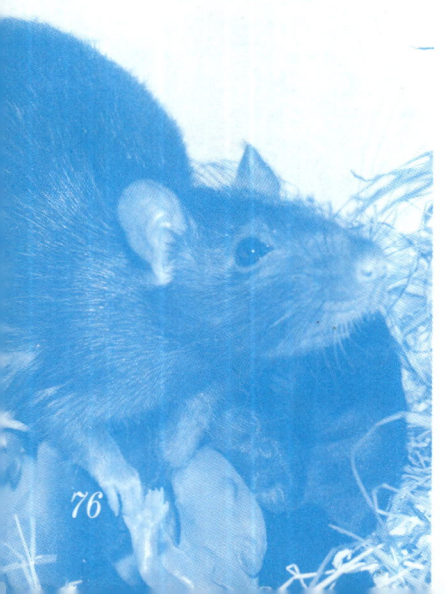

Fancy rats have become accepted as great pets for young and old alike

RATS

Acquiring a rat

Having decided that you want a fancy rat of your own, you now need to know where to obtain one. Plenty of pet shops sell fancy rats, but it is always best to pay a visit to a rat fancier who is more than likely to have some young rats – called kittens – for sale. Alternatively, visit a fancy rat show, where there are usually some kittens for sale.

The healthy fancy rat should have a clean coat, bright eyes, erect ears, a long, whiplash tail, and a sleek body. The rat should be alert and curious, not overly afraid of scrutiny by its prospective new owner, although bear in mind that all young animals are nervous of strangers.

Fancy rats may be kept individually, in pairs or in larger groups. If your lifestyle means you are at home for most of the day and can devote plenty of time to a rat on a one-to-one basis, then a single rat is fine, but never ideal. They are gregarious, sociable animals and enjoy the company of their own kind. So, particularly if you are out of the house for the best part of the day, two rats – ideally of the same sex to prevent unwanted litters – will keep each other company.

There are plenty of well-designed rat cages on the market

Housing

There are plenty of well-designed rat cages on the market, which can be bought from any good pet shop. The best ones are part metal or plastic, and part glass, preferably as tall as practicable: rats are quite athletic and enjoy climbing. Certainly the cage should be high enough to allow the rat to stand on its hind legs, as they frequently do.

Alternatively, an old aquarium tank, fitted with a strong wire-mesh lid makes an ideal home for a pair of fancy rats. The minimum cage size recommended for a pair of rats is 90cm x 30cm x30cm (36in x 12in x 12in). For large groups of rats, tall cages may be constructed out of aviary panels, although it is vital to ensure that the cage is provided with a thick, solid base, to prevent the rats from gnawing their way out!

RATS

The floor of the cage should be covered with wood shavings, rather than sawdust, which is too fine and may be breathed in by the rats, causing respiratory problems. Bedding isn't necessary, but, if you wish to provide it, hay or shredded paper is best. Newspaper should not be used, as the print is poisonous.

Being athletic, energetic creatures, rats enjoy being off the floor and climbing around. Place a couple of little platforms inside the cage or put a clean branch inside for the rats to run up and down and chew. Swings and ropes suspended from the cage roof or lid will also prove popular.

Like most rodents, rats love chewing, so cardboard boxes and tubes are ideal for this purpose. A small block of softwood for your rats to gnaw will help keep their incisor teeth honed down and dissuade them from chewing anything they should not.

ACCESSORIES CHECK LIST

- Strong food bowls
- A suitably sized cage for two rats
- Water bottle
- Toys and items to chew
- Ropes and swings

Feeding

Fancy rats, like their wild counterparts, are true omnivores and have quite cosmopolitan tastes. Their staple diet should consist of a dry mix of flaked maize, crushed peas, biscuit and pellets. However, be careful to avoid mixes which contain a large number of sunflower seeds or peanuts, as these are very rich in protein and can give rats sores and spots through a protein overdose, which is a very common ailment experienced by many pet rats. Every second or third day, the basic diet can be supplemented with vegetables and fruit, favourites being carrot, swede, celery, cucumber, tomatoes, apples and grapes. Citrus fruits are to be avoided, as these are far too acidic for a rat's stomach.

These rats will enjoy table scraps, such as spaghetti, potato, sweetcorn, chips, cooked vegetables and a little meat. Indeed, meat bones are also a valuable addition to the rat's diet, as they will not only eat the meat, but also gnaw the bones, exercising their teeth, and eat the marrow, which is good for them. In short, fancy rats leave very little food behind!

Fancy rats also have a sweet tooth and will welcome chocolate drops as an occasional treat. Be careful not to over-indulge

Fancy rats are true omnivores and have quite cosmopolitan tastes

RATS

them, however, as obesity is a common problem in rats. Fresh water should always be available, preferably supplied via a gravity water bottle.

Exercise and daily care

Being such active and curious creatures, fancy rats require regular exercise and plenty of attention from their owners. They may be tamed easily by the simple process of proffering a tasty titbit and quietly talking to them in a soothing voice. After this, rats may be easily handled, the best method being to grip the animal around its midriff, gently but firmly, and then place it on the crook of one's arm. They should never be lifted by the tail unless absolutely necessary and even then they should only be gripped at the base of the tail, never the tip, as the tail can easily 'skin' and cause considerable pain to the rat.

Fancy rats can be taken out of their cages and allowed to run on the sofa or even on the floor, but be careful that they don't escape into the hessian under furniture – a favourite rodent trick – or chew through electrical cables!

With regular handling, many rats can become very tame and learn to come when called. If you like performing pets, then it may also be possible to teach your fancy rat a few tricks by using treats as a reward. Some have even been known to learn to retrieve small objects thrown for them to fetch.

Hygiene-wise, fancy rats are very clean animals, but, like any rodent, they do have a distinctive odour which is very noticeable if their cage is not cleaned out often enough. The cage should be cleaned out at least once a week and thoroughly washed and sterilised every two months. Any uneaten food should be removed after a day or two before it becomes mouldy.

Breeding

Rats are, like most rodents, highly prolific breeders, largely because they become sexually mature at a young age. In the domestic environment, the breeding of fancy rats must be carefully regulated.

Rats are, like most rodents, highly prolific breeders, because they become sexually mature at a young age

RATS

The female rat, the doe, has a five-day oestrus cycle when she will be receptive to the male, the buck. Usually, this is noticeable by the doe being very flighty and excitable and then adopting a passive stance if touched on the flanks.

The buck and doe may be housed in a normal cage and left together for a week or even two, which will allow for mating to take place when the doe comes on heat. The doe will show signs of pregnancy by a distinct swelling of the abdomen, at which point the pair can be split up. The doe should be given extra food and plenty of bedding to allow her to make a nest for her litter.

Gestation lasts between 21 and 23 days, with the litter size averaging between seven and ten babies – known as kittens. The kittens are born naked, blind and deaf. They emit high-pitched squeaks so that the doe can locate them easily. The doe will be quite protective of her litter, so it is best not to attempt to handle them for at least three days, making sure that the doe is kept in a quiet place with nothing to cause her undue stress. It is rare for a rat to eat her litter, but not unheard of if she feels they are under threat.

If the doe trusts you and settles, you may gently handle the litter when they are a few days old, making sure to rub your hands in the wood shavings to acquire the cage smell so as not to worry the doe. A few minutes' gentle handling will go some way towards making the kittens tame.

At around five days of age, the fur begins to develop and the first signs of colour and markings are visible. By ten days, the kittens are fully furred, their ears are open and their incisor teeth have broken through. They will now start to eat solid food, which the doe brings into the nest for them. It is a good idea to provide them with bread and milk, which provides calcium, along with plenty of their regular diet.

By 14 days of age, their eyes have opened and the kittens explore the cage, finding food for themselves. As they grow, they indulge in madcap games of play fighting that help them establish their own pecking order, as dominance plays a great part in rat colony behaviour.

With regular handling, many rats can become very tame and learn to come when called

RATS

At the age of six weeks, the kittens should be weaned and removed to a separate cage. At this stage, sexing them should be easy, and bucks and does should be split up into single sex groups, as they can achieve sexual maturity as early as eight weeks of age. After this, you can select which kittens you wish to keep and which you wish to sell or rehome.

Showing and varieties

There are many different rat clubs in the UK and the US, most of which will be affiliated to the main, national societies. Attending rat shows is great fun, not only from a competitive point of view, but because it allows you to meet other fancy rat lovers.

The rats themselves are nowadays bred in many different colour varieties, such as pink-eyed white (albino), silver fawn, argente, cinnamon, cinnamon pearl, Himalayan and Siamese (like the Siamese cat), while marked varieties include hooded, capped and variegated (a spotted rat, rather akin to a dalmatian dog). There is even a curly-coated variety known as rex. In America, hairless and tail-less rats are also recognised varieties – although these are not to everyone's taste and are prone to hereditary health problems.

One of the latest new varieties is the Dumbo rat. This variety was developed in the US and has gained popularity in the UK and throughout Europe. The animals themselves are perfectly normal, healthy fancy rats, bred in any colour or coat type, but with larger ears than normal, set further back on their heads. The Dumbo appellation refers to the size of the ears, the variety being named after the Disney cartoon elephant.

If you like performing pets, then it may also be possible to teach your fancy rat a few tricks by using treats as a reward

HEALTH CARE

- Fancy rats are quite robust, hardy rodents generally. Their most common ailments are usually skin problems and obesity, invariably caused by too much rich food.

- Respiratory problems are more common in older rats, but can easily arise if the rat is kept in a draughty, damp or cold environment. Standard room temperature of 16–18°C is best for them.

- Old rats are also very prone to tumours and, although it is possible to operate on some rats to remove a tumour, there is a strong likelihood that further tumours will swiftly develop.

- Properly cared for, fancy rats can enjoy a happy, healthy and active lifespan of up to three years, averaging around 22 months.

MICE

Mice – you either love them or loathe them. Whatever your personal feelings towards them, however, you've got to admire their tenacity. As a species, these small rodents have proved themselves extremely successful – no mean feat for a scavenging species – and have made the transition from vermin to family pet.

History of mice

Mus musculus, the house mouse, originated in Asia and quickly spread out and colonised the world alongside humans. Wherever humans settled, there the mouse settled. Every town, village and city in the world has colonies of mice within its dwellings, underground railways, grain stores, warehouses and factories. But mice are also much maligned animals. Because of their scavenging and gnawing activities, mice have been classed as vermin.

However, there is a certain fascination about mice. We may despise their scavenging, but we idolise them through literature and popular culture. Quite apart from all of this, domestic – or fancy – mice make excellent pets for young and old alike, and have long been prized as exhibition livestock. True, mice may not be the most interesting of pets, compared, say, to a gerbil or a rat, which are much more interactive with their owners, but they are among the cheapest and easiest to keep.

Mice were among the first small livestock to be domesticated as pets, probably due, in part, to their small size and ease of handling. Ancient woodcuts and illustrations from royal palaces of China and Japan show what are obviously distinctly marked varieties of fancy mice, along with children handling their pet mice.

Mice had been kept as pets in the UK for many, many years before the idea of a formal 'mouse fancy' was even mooted. It is certain that fancy mice were being bred in different colours and markings prior to 1892, when the first classes for mice were laid on at a show in Oxford. The classes attracted a surprisingly large number of fancy mice – shown mainly as curios by rabbit, cavy and cat fanciers. This led to several interested mouse breeders

MICE

getting together and exchanging mice. More classes were staged at other livestock shows and mice were hailed as 'the coming fancy'. By 1895, the number of mouse fanciers had grown sufficiently to enable them to found a formalised mouse club. Thus, it was in December 1895 that the National Mouse Club was founded, which exists to this day and to which a number of area mouse clubs are affiliated.

Meanwhile, mice have been taken up as pets and exhibition animals around the world, particularly in the US, where there are several mouse clubs.

Acquiring a mouse

Being gregarious animals, mice like the company of their own kind. To this end, a pair of mice is the perfect arrangement. However, mice are also incredibly prolific, so, assuming you don't want wall-to-wall baby mice, it is best to opt for a single sex pair. Females (does) are the best pairing. Males (bucks) will live together quite amicably, but their urine contains a particularly strong odour, not present to the same degree in does, so it is important to make sure their cage is kept especially clean!

Most pet shops stock mice of various varieties, but if you are intent on obtaining the best specimens with a view possibly to exhibiting them at shows, then it is always best to visit a breeder. Even the best mice are relatively cheap to buy – as well as being cheap to keep.

Being gregarious animals, mice like the company of their own kind

Housing

There are several perfectly suitable cages for mice available from any good pet shop. These vary in design between the standard plastic bottom and wire canopy affair to metal and glass constructions, with numerous ladders and pathways leading to upper levels. Alternatively, an old aquarium tank makes an ideal home if fitted with a close gauge wire lid. The ideal size of cage for a pair of mice should measure 40cm x 20cm x 20cm (18in x 8in x 8in).

MICE

Mice are easily satisfied creatures, but they do enjoy climbing and taking a spin on an exercise wheel. When providing such a wheel, remember that the solid variety is preferable to the open-spoked variety, in which mice may sustain tail injuries.

Wood shavings or sawdust should be spread on the floor of the cage. Hay is the best bedding, as the mice will also eat this and it will provide essential roughage in their diet.

The cardboard tubes from inside toilet rolls make fun tunnels for the mice to run through and also provide them with something to chew on, as, being rodents, they have a natural tendency to gnaw.

Today, there are well over 50 different varieties of fancy mice to tempt the would-be fancier and pet keeper alike

Feeding

Again, mice are very easy and cheap to feed. Their staple diet should consist of flaked maize and crushed dried peas. Avoid mixes that contain too many protein-rich sunflower seeds and peanuts, as these can cause skin sores in mice.

Vegetables such as lettuce, cabbage and carrot, along with fruits such as apples and grapes may be given as a supplement to the main diet every third day or so. A few table scraps may also be given in moderation, potatoes and spaghetti being especially welcomed. Other useful supplements are brown bread and milk once a week, especially nutritious for young mice and helpful to the development of strong bones.

Mice are very easy and cheap to feed. They only need to be fed once a day

Mice need only be fed once a day. All uneaten fruit, vegetables or table scraps should be removed from the cage daily at each feeding time. Fresh drinking water should always be available, provided via a gravity water bottle.

Care and maintenance

When first purchased, mice are prone to be a little nervous. Let them get used to their new home for a couple of days, then start offering them titbits and stroking them gently.

MICE

Handling mice is easy. They may be gently lifted by the tail, although remember to grasp the root, not the tip. Transfer the mouse to your forearm where it will either sit happily or scamper up to your shoulder.

When tame, mice can be allowed to run free for a few minutes each day. But remember to supervise them carefully and ensure that they don't escape into any holes or chew electrical wires. A mouse is capable of squeezing into an improbably small hole, so be warned!

Their cage should be cleaned out at least once a week and thoroughly disinfected every second or third month.

Sadly, mice are not the longest-lived of animals and their average life span is around 18 months, although some particularly robust individuals can live to two years or slightly more.

Mice have a high fertility rate; a short gestation period and they reach maturity quickly

Breeding

Mice are counted among the most prolific of all animals. They have a high fertility rate, a short gestation period and they reach maturity quickly. Naturally, this goes along with the fact that they are such short-lived animals.

Mice reach sexual maturity between six and eight weeks of age, but it is best not to breed from them too young. The usual breeding formula is to 'run' a buck with two or more does, but there is a little more to successful breeding than simply letting nature take its course. Breeding adults must be selected with a number of important factors in mind: size, stamina, type and, of course, the required variety.

Initially, the buck should be housed on his own, with does introduced to him as required. Ovulation in mice lasts between four and six days, with heat lasting for up to 12 hours. At this time, the doe is at the peak of fertility and the buck will quickly mate with her.

The babies grow quickly and, after a few days, their ears open and they squeak loudly

MICE

Pregnancy is soon noticeable, with the doe's body swelling greatly, especially over the flanks. At this point the doe is said to be 'in kindle' and can be removed to her own cage to give birth to her litter. Does have a condition known as postpartum oestrus, where they will go into heat immediately after their litter is born, whereupon they are receptive to mating. To be pregnant while raising a litter will debilitate the doe, so it is always best to remove her from the buck before the litter is born.

Gestation lasts between 18 and 21 days. During this time, provide the doe with extra bedding for her to make her nest, and extra food — especially bread and milk — to build up her bodily reserves. The litter is usually born in the evening or early dawn hours. The babies are born naked, blind and deaf, able only to suckle from their mother. It is best not to disturb the nest for the first two or three days to allow the doe to settle down.

The babies grow quickly and, after a few days, their ears open and they squeak loudly. Fur begins to grow at around four days, with the markings on patterned varieties becoming apparent at this time.

The eyes open at 14 days and the babies then begin to scurry around. They will have started to nibble at solid food by now, so make sure to provide extra food for them. A bread and milk mixture is an ideal supplement to give them extra calcium and vitamin B to promote growth. The litter should be weaned by 28 days and the babies split into single sex groups.

Sexing mice is easy, the best method is to hold the mouse up by the tail and inspect the groin area. The distance between the urethra and the anus is greater in bucks than in does. Does also have two rows of nipples, which are often visible at a young age.

The doe, having raised her litter, should now be allowed to rest for a week or so. Carefully used, a doe can produce up to 10 litters in her lifetime. The buck usually remains virile until the day he dies, but, generally speaking, virility and fertility in each sex will fade after 12 to 14 months of age.

> **ACCESSORIES CHECK LIST**
> - Water bottle
> - A suitably sized cage for two mice
> - Strong food bowls
> - Toys and items to chew

Handling mice is easy. They may be gently lifted by the tail — remember to grasp the root, not the tip

MICE

Showing and varieties

In the century since the formation of the National Mouse Club, many different varieties of fancy mice have been developed and official standards of excellence drawn up.

Today, there are well over 50 different varieties of fancy mice to tempt the would-be fancier and pet keeper alike. Varieties include fawn, red, black, dove, argente and silver, while the more exotic varieties include Dutch, rump white, variegated, broken marked, banded and Himalayan. Another popular group are the tan varieties, where the mouse has a deep tan colour on its belly, in contrast with a standard colour on the top half of the animal.

For coat variation, you can choose from rex and astrexes (curly-coated), longhaired and even longhaired astrex. Also, every variety can be bred with a satin coat, which shines like gloss. Naturally, cross breeding turns up any number of mongrel varieties, which may not be suitable for showing, but which are perfectly suitable as ordinary pets.

Shows are an ideal place to meet like-minded mouse fans and the best approach is to contact the national mouse organisation and they will then put you in touch with your local mouse club. There are generally mouse shows staged at least once a month, sometimes more, so there's plenty of scope for contact with other mouse lovers.

Mice are easily satisfied creatures, but they do enjoy climbing and taking a spin on an exercise wheel

MICE

COMMON AILMENTS

Mice are pretty robust and healthy for such small creatures. Generally speaking, if they are well fed and kept at the correct temperature, they enjoy good health. The most common health problems your mice may encounter are:

- Mites: Small, fur-dwelling parasites can be brought in with untreated hay and wood shavings or even by other, infected mice. The mouse can be treated simply by dipping it carefully in an anti-parasite solution, prescribed by a vet – simply take care to cover the mouse's eyes and ears with your hand. One dunk should be enough to cure the problem.

- Diarrhoea: As with most animals, the symptoms are obvious and smelly. It tends to mean that your mouse has eaten too much green food. Simply cut out all vegetables and fruit from the mouse's diet for a few days and provide it with plain, dry food mixture (and fresh drinking water, of course). The condition should soon correct itself, after which time green food can be fed again, in small quantities. Sometimes diarrhoea can be caused by a bacterial infection, so, if symptoms persist, seek veterinary advice.

- Colds: Mice are susceptible to changes in temperature and can catch respiratory infections quite easily. With a cold they will have a runny nose, sore eyes and poor coat condition, and will display general lethargy. Isolate any infected mice in a warmer area with extra bedding and give them plenty of nutritious extras, such as bread and milk. Cod liver oil added to the food can help restore them to better health.

HAMSTERS

Of all the pet rodents, the Syrian (or golden) hamster, *Mesocricetus auratus*, ranks as one of the most popular. In fact, it's quite surprising that the hamster became a pet at all, given that they were quite rare in their native Syria during the early years of the last century.

The name 'hamster' is derived from the German word *hamstern*, meaning 'to hoard'. This is something they do extremely well, as one of this small rodent's most endearing features is its elastic-like cheek pouches in which it can temporarily store, and thereby transport, large quantities of food.

Hamsters are easy to keep and cheap to maintain. However, they do have one big drawback as a pet, they hate each other! Syrian hamsters must not be kept in pairs, even single sex pairs, as they will fight to the death. Apart from coming together for carefully supervised mating sessions, hamsters must live solitary lives, which suits them just fine.

History of hamsters

In 1930, Professor Israel Aharoni of the Hebrew University in Jerusalem undertook an expedition to capture some hamsters on behalf of his colleague at the university, parasitologist Saul Adler, for use in his research into the prevalent disease, *leishmaniasis*. On 12th April 1930, Aharoni unearthed a nest containing one female hamster and her litter of 11 young in the Aleppo region of Syria. These were duly taken back to the Hebrew University and presented to Adler. The mother and all but four of the young died, but this first colony bred actively and gave rise to 365 descendants in the first year! Adler distributed several captive-bred Syrian hamsters to other laboratories around the world in order to spread the gene pool. In this way, the first hamsters arrived in London Zoo in 1931, while a similar colony reached the US in 1938.

HAMSTERS

In the late 1940s, captive-bred hamsters began to find their way into pet shops and, in a very short space of time, they were established as favourite pets and sought-after show animals. Apart from a further capture of wild Syrian hamsters in May and June 1971, by American Michael R Murphy, as well as further captures during more recent years, every pet Syrian hamster alive today is almost certainly descended from the original Aleppo litter.

Acquiring a hamster

Needless to say, being such a popular pet, hamsters are very easy to come by. They are sold in most pet shops and specialist breeders often have excess stock for sale, due to the fairly large litters that a hamster can give birth to.

Nearly every pet hamster is descended from the original Aleppo litter

Although the Syrian hamster is most commonly known as the golden hamster, on account of its natural pigmentation (which is more ruddy brown and white than golden), it is available in a truly breathtaking range of colours, markings and varieties. Typical colours include golden, cinnamon, cream, albino, various shades of grey, black, dove, sable and chocolate. Marked varieties include dominant spot, tortoiseshell and banded, as well as combinations of these. Hamsters also have several different coat types apart from the usual short smooth coat, including long-hair, rex, a beautiful, shiny coated satin, or a combination of any of these types.

Housing

There are numerous types of hamster cages available on the pet market, many of which come in weird and wonderful, highly complex designs involving tubes and tunnels. However, some of these are inherently dangerous – a large hamster can easily get stuck in a small plastic tunnel and suffocate. The best type of cage is one with a full or partial wire canopy and a sturdy metal or plastic base.

HAMSTERS

The minimum size should be 40cm x 24cm x 20cm (16in x 12in x 8in). The floor of the cage should be covered with wood shavings purchased from a pet shop. Shredded paper – also pet shop bought - is best for the hamster's bedding. Avoid fibre-based nylon or cotton wool type bedding as the strands can easily become wrapped around the hamster's toes or even clog its cheeks, causing injury or death.

The hamster's cage should be cleaned out and all wood shavings and bedding replaced once a week. It is also a good idea to wash and disinfect the cage thoroughly every two or three months, as germs can harbour in cage corners.

The bulk of a hamster's diet should consist of dry hamster mix. Vegetables and fruit may be given every second or third day

Feeding

The bulk of a hamster's diet should consist of dry hamster mix, readily available through pet shops. The mix should ideally contain flaked maize, crushed dried peas, wheat and a small quantity of sunflower seeds and peanuts. Dry dog or cat food can be added to the mix to raise the protein level. Vegetables and fruit may be given every second or third day as a supplement to the dry mix. Carrot, lettuce, celery, apple and tomato are relished. Avoid citrus fruits such as oranges, however, as these are too acidic for the hamster's stomach. Hamsters will also relish table scraps, such as bread, pasta, cooked potatoes, sweetcorn and peas, but avoid spicy or hot foods.

The food should be placed in a sturdy earthenware bowl, which cannot be tipped over. As hamsters hoard their food, they will very often build up quite a large store of uneaten food in one corner of the cage, usually near their nest. Carefully remove all uneaten vegetables and table scraps after a day or they will begin to go mouldy. Of course, any uneaten food will be disposed of with the weekly cage clean out, too. Fresh drinking water should always be available and is best provided by a gravity water bottle fixed to the cage bars.

ACCESSORIES

- Good quality cage
- Strong earthenware or metal food bowl
- Gravity water bottle
- Exercise wheel
- Exercise ball
- Grooming brush and small comb for long-haired varieties

HAMSTERS

Breeding

Hamsters, like most rodents, can be quite prolific breeders. However, unlike most other rodents, they are somewhat more complex when it comes to the actual process of breeding, which you must carefully supervise.

As mentioned above, Syrian hamsters should not be kept in pairs, so getting the timing of the breeding right is crucial. The female hamster comes into heat every four days and only then in the evening. During the winter months she may not become pregnant at all if she is kept in a cool environment. To check whether or not the female is in heat, gently scratch her back. If she is in heat, she will assume the mating position, literally 'freezing', with her tail erect and eyes half closed, ready for a male.

If the female is in heat, place her in the male's cage, or in a neutral cage – never in the female's cage, as, heat or not, she will see this as an invasion of her territory and will attack the male. Mating will take place several times over the next 15 minutes to half an hour. Never leave the pair entirely alone as they need to be supervised, in case the female feels that she has had enough and starts to attack the male.

Hamsters have one of the shortest gestation periods of small mammals, just 16 to 17 days. If the female is pregnant, her condition may not become clear until around 12 days after mating, as her abdomen swells with the growing babies inside her. If she is carrying a small litter, there may be no obvious change in appearance at all. The female should be provided with extra food during this time to build up her bodily reserves and help her to produce plenty of milk for her litter. Her cage should be thoroughly cleaned out a day or two before day 16 of her pregnancy and extra bedding provided for her to make a nest.

Ensure that the cage is in a good location, neither too warm nor too cold, and preferably somewhere quiet so that the female will not be disturbed by people constantly coming near the cage. A nervous female may kill and eat her babies in order to 'protect' them. If a female who has just given birth starts to

Hamsters are popular show pets, and can be shown in special small show cages

HAMSTERS

panic and attack or move her babies, cover the cage with a blanket or towel and leave her alone for at least 24 hours. This will usually help her settle. It is vital to ensure that she has a good supply of protein rich food (such as canned cat food or baby food) and water in her cage, as, again she may kill her babies if she is not well fed.

The babies are born blind, deaf and naked, like most rodent offspring, although they grow and develop rapidly. The average litter size is eight, although much larger litters are not uncommon.

By the fourth day after birth, the babies will have developed a fine covering of fur and their pigmentation and markings will be clear. They will already have small teeth and their ears will have unfolded. By day eight, they will be nibbling at solid food, although still suckling from their mother. At this time it is possible to sex the babies, the females having two very clear rows of nipples visible on their bellies.

If the mother is calm, she will allow you to gently handle her offspring at this stage, which helps in the process of taming them. Before attempting to handle the babies, first rub your hands in some urine soaked shavings from the cage, to mask your human scent. Also, remove the female from the cage. If at all unsure, do not touch the babies until they have left the nest at around 14 days of age, when their eyes have opened.

At the age of three weeks, the babies are fully furred, their eyes open and they resemble miniature adults. Extra food should be provided. A little tinned cat food and some bread and milk make a tasty and nutritious supplement to the family's diet. At the age of four weeks, the babies may be weaned and removed from their mother's cage, as she will now be very fed up with them and may even begin to attack them if they attempt to suckle from her.

At five weeks the sexes should be split up into two groups in separate cages, as they can become sexually active at this time and it is not unknown for female hamsters to become pregnant at this age. By six or seven weeks at the latest, the babies should have their own cages or have been sold or re-homed as required.

Baby hamsters are born blind, deaf and naked. By the fourth day after birth, they will have developed fur

HAMSTERS

General maintainence and exercise

Hamsters are nocturnal by nature, although many will adapt their lifestyles to suit that of their owners and become more active by day.

Hamsters can be quite energetic in short bursts of intense activity. The cheapest way to amuse your hamster is to save cardboard tubes from toilet or kitchen rolls. These are ideal for the hamster to chew, thus exercising its sharp incisor teeth.

Exercise wheels are a perfect way for a hamster to get exercise and they will spend many happy hours trundling round and round. Many cages are sold complete with exercise wheels, but do not use a wheel which is less than 13cm (5in) in diameter, as a smaller wheel will cause strain on the hamster's back. Wheels are not very suitable for long-haired hamsters, as their coats can become entangled in the spokes.

Plastic exercise balls are ideal for long-haired hamsters or, indeed, any type of hamster. Simply place the hamster in the ball and let it run around, carefully supervised, of course, especially if there are larger pets around such as cats and dogs. Some balls have a small stand, so that the hamster can trundle the ball round and round like an exercise wheel without actually going anywhere. However, always be careful not to let the hamster remain in the ball for more than 20 minutes at a time, as even the best ventilated exercise balls can make a hamster feel too hot after a while.

Hamsters can become very tame with a little patience – offering them titbits of food from your fingers is a good way to gain their confidence. Try to avoid plunging your hand into the cage and just grabbing the hamster, especially if it is asleep, because even the tamest hamster will be startled and rather put out by this and give you a nasty nip!

They can be handled easily enough, simply by being held round their midriff with one hand and transferred onto the palm of your other hand or onto your forearm. They can be stroked gently and respond to being spoken to quietly.

→ *Continued on page 105*

Exercise wheels are a perfect way for a hamster to get exercise

Top: Left, white Persian. Right, Russian blue kitten. Bottom: Left, short-haired red tabby. Right, Somali kittens

Top: *Left, colourpoint (seal tabby point). Right, red tabby kittens.* **Bottom**: *Left, Dalmatian. Right, Sheep dog*

Top: Left, mongrel. Right, springer spaniel. Bottom: Left, Dobermann, chihuahua. Right, yorkshire terrier

*Top: Left, gerbil. Right, mouse. **Bottom**: Left, rabbit and its baby. Right, baby yellow hamsters*

Top: Left, ferrets. Right, hamster and exercise wheel. Bottom: Left, mouse. Right, chinchilla

Top: Left, black and white mouse. Right, gerbil. *Bottom*: Left, Abyssinian guinea pig. Right, rat and wheel

*Top: Left, scarlet macaws. Right, eclectus. **Bottom:** Left, green-naped lorikeet. Right, cockatoos*

Top: Left, royal gramma. Right, harlequin tusk fish. Bottom: Left, Undulatus trigger fish. Right, lionfish

HAMSTERS

 *Continued from page 96*

Hamsters need very little actual grooming or cleaning, as they are very clean animals. However, long-haired hamsters might need a bit of help with their coats and to this end, they will need regular gentle brushing with a small, soft brush and a small comb to tease out the knots or any pieces of wood shavings in their coat.

Showing

Hamsters are very popular show animals and there are many local, regional and specialist hamster clubs, which will stage regular shows. It is best to find the national hamster society via specialist magazines or the internet. Make contact with them and they will put you in touch with your nearest club. Attending shows can be a great way of meeting fellow hamster enthusiasts and, of course, maybe even acquiring more hamsters!

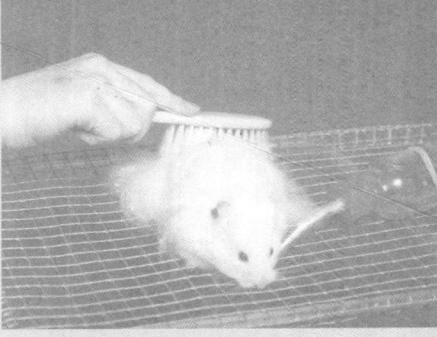

Every hamster should be given a gravity water bottle and some occasional grooming

WHAT IS IT?

Many owners (and some vets too) are worried when they see what appear to be lumps or sores on the hamster's flanks. No need to worry! These are scent glands, which are very noticeable in some hamsters. The female's glands produce a musky odour, designed to announce the hamster's presence to other hamsters, usually for mating purposes. The glands can exude a sticky discharge, especially if the hamster licks them to stimulate production of the discharge. The glands usually subside after a few days and dry up, with no ill-effects to the hamster whatsoever.

GERBILS

Gerbils are one of the most popular small pets in the UK and have been since their introduction to the pet market in the 1960s. There is more than one species of gerbil to be found in pet shops and even jirds, their larger cousins, have a high degree of popularity.

The gerbil is from the subfamily known as *Gerbillinae*, which is divided into three groups, *Gerbillus*, *Meriones* and *Tatara*. Mouse-like jirds, such as the pallid gerbil, belong to the Gerbillus group. The Mongolian gerbil, *Meriones unguiculatus*, is the species most commonly referred to as a gerbil, and kept as a pet, although being part of the Meriones group it is in fact a small jird.

History of gerbils

In 1866, the famous naturalist, Pere David, discovered a colony of gerbils while on a collecting trip in Mongolia. He made many entries about these 'Jerboas', as he called them, observing how they hopped along or stood on their hind legs, looking about them with great curiosity. This is one of the gerbil's most endearing qualities as a pet.

In the mid-1930s, a number of Mongolian gerbils were captured and sent to Japan to form a breeding colony in the Japanese Central Laboratory for Experimental Animals. Some time later, in 1954, 11 pairs were sent from there to a medical research centre in the US. In time, a number of offspring made their way into the hands of commercial animal breeders and from here into schools and pet shops. In a very short space of time the gerbil was the top pet in America. In the early 1960s, several specimens were exported to the UK, where they quickly became popular. Part of their appeal is that gerbils are sociable animals and may be kept in single sex pairs of similar age.

GERBILS

ACCESSORIES CHECK LIST

- Cage
- Heavy food bowl
- Water bottle
- Toys
- Jam jar to make a burrow
- Extra wood shavings or peat for burrowing
- Exercise wheel

Housing

Gerbils are very easy to house, as there are many suitable, purpose-designed cages available in good pet shops. Although typical cages with bars, designed for hamsters, are acceptable for gerbils, there is the disadvantage that gerbils excel in kicking lots of wood shavings out of the cage. An aquarium tank is the ideal home for gerbils, giving good all-round vision and protection, with solid walls out of which no wood shavings can be kicked! As gerbils are capable of jumping quite high, a strong wire lid for the aquarium, suitably weighed down, is essential. A cage measuring 60cm x 30cm x 30cm (24in x 12in x 12in) is ideal for a pair of gerbils to live happily.

Material to cover the floor of the cage is easy: wood shavings or peat are the ideal materials. Gerbils love to burrow, so plenty of floor covering is appreciated. To this end, an empty jam jar in the cage has great appeal for gerbils, as they will pile shavings or peat into this and then furiously burrow into it, just as if they were digging a tunnel.

Clean branches to climb, hide between or chew are also appreciated, as are a number of cardboard tubes, which will be chewed to shreds in a very short space of time. The best nesting material is clean fresh hay, which can also be eaten and will provide roughage in their diet. Alternatively, shredded paper purchased from a pet shop makes ideal bedding and will be merrily weaved into a typically elaborate gerbil nest.

Feeding

Gerbils are very easy to feed. Their basic diet should be a dry rodent mixture, comprising crushed oats, flaked maize and crushed dried peas. Avoid too many sunflower seeds and peanuts, as these are very rich in protein and can lead to skin problems and obesity if eaten in large quantities.

Vegetables and fruit may be given every second or third day as a supplement to the standard diet. Carrots, celery, lettuce and apples are greatly appreciated, although citrus fruits should be avoided because of their high acidity content. In the wild,

GERBILS

insects form a large part of the gerbil's diet, so they may take mealworms, although these should be given in moderation, due to their high protein content.

Like most active rodents, gerbils have a propensity for overturning their food bowls, so the heavier the better. However, they also enjoy digging and foraging for their food, so it won't hurt to sprinkle a little bit of dry food on to the wood shavings or peat and let the gerbils bury it and then dig it up again. It all adds interest to their lives and provides mental, as well as physical, stimulus.

Although gerbils are desert animals and can go without water for some days if need be, fresh drinking water should always be available, provided by a gravity water bottle.

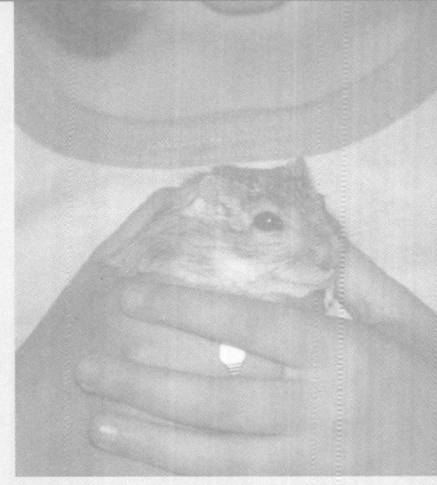

The standard gerbil is a sandy brown and white colour

Acquiring a gerbil

Being so popular, gerbils are usually to be found in most pet shops and, nowadays, there is an extremely good choice of colours and markings. Occasionally, pet shops may sell pallid, or Egyptian, gerbils, which are more mouse-like than Mongolian gerbils (see above) and are often only available in their usual golden brown colour. Their requirements are much the same as Mongolian gerbils.

A single gerbil will easily become bored and quite stressed, so it is best to have a pair

Breeders often have excess stock for sale and usually will be able to provide a wider choice of gerbil varieties than are found in pet shops.

The standard gerbil is a sandy brown and white colour, but, over the years many more varieties have been developed, including albino, black, dove, argente, cream, patched and many more.

Gerbils are very sociable animals and enjoy each other's company. A single gerbil will easily become bored and quite stressed, so it is best to have a pair. Obviously, a single sex pair prevents unwanted litters, although, curiously, true pairs will often take a voluntary break between litters, so they are not as prolific breeders as many other small rodents.

GERBILS

When you bring your gerbils home, leave them to explore their new home and get used to your comings and goings, and the sounds of the house. They are extremely curious animals. This natural curiosity will soon lead to them running up to greet you every time you come near their cage and swiftly adapting to their new surroundings.

General care and maintenance

Gerbils are naturally energetic animals and very inquisitive, so will enjoy being allowed out of their cage for exercise and to explore – but, be careful that they are supervised and cannot escape under furniture or into nooks and crannies, or chew electrical cables! They will soon become tame and may be handled easily by putting your hand around their bodies or by gently grasping their tail close to the root and then transferring the gerbil to your arm or the palm of your hand. Never pick a gerbil up by the top of its tail as the tuft of fur will come off, a natural defence mechanism to escape predators in the wild, but, once lost, the tuft will never grow back. Exercise wheels may also be given to gerbils, but the solid type are best, so their tails will not get caught between spokes.

Gerbils are naturally nocturnal, but, like most pet rodents, they will adjust their lifestyle according to their owners and will be more active when people are about. Gerbils are generally very robust and live slightly longer than most other rodent species, their average lifespan ranging between three and four years.

Every gerbil species shares a fascinating habit of 'drumming' with their hind legs when nervous or excited. This happens particularly when gerbils live in colonies – as in the wild – when one individual is posted as a lookout and alerts the whole colony to the presence of danger by drumming its hind legs. Very often, pet gerbils will drum in anticipation of food or exercise when their owner approaches their cage. Usually the drumming ceases once the gerbils have established that there is no threat in the vicinity.

GERBILS

Breeding

Like most small rodents, gerbils reach sexual maturity at a young age – usually between nine and twelve weeks. As mentioned above, true pairs don't breed constantly and have the added bonus of being very calm in the presence of a litter. The male gerbil may be left in the cage when the female is nursing the litter and he will even take a turn in the nursing duties himself.

The female has a regular oestrus cycle, which lasts for four days, and mating occurs pretty much when the gerbils feel like it. The gestation period averages 24 days and the young are born blind, deaf and naked. The average litter size is four to six, although larger and smaller litters aren't unusual.

The female will most likely come into heat immediately after giving birth – a process known as post-partum oestrus – and the male will mate with her. However, the fertilized eggs in the female's uterus will not immediately be implanted into the uterus wall, thereby delaying the development of a new litter and extending gestation for several weeks until the first litter has been weaned.

The babies develop quickly, with their fur appearing between five and seven days and their eyes and ears opening fully soon after. At about two weeks, the babies are wandering out of the nest, often being picked up and carried back by their mother, and soon after this they will start nibbling at food, although they will still suckle from their mother until the age of four weeks.

It would be helpful to provide a bowl of bread and milk for the growing youngsters and maybe some tasty titbits in their food to encourage them to eat. However, in general, young gerbils need very little in the way of 'extras' to help them along.

The young can be weaned at four to five weeks of age and split into single sex groups. Sexing gerbils is quite easy, as males have a more pronounced groin area, while the female's genitalia are closer to their anus.

Gerbils are naturally energetic and very inquisitive animals

Showing

- Gerbils have become prized as show animals, although, the gerbil fancy is not as large or widespread as those of other small rodents.

- Check out the address of the national gerbil club for details about local groups and forthcoming shows.

CHINCHILLAS

It wasn't so very long ago that the chinchilla used to be exclusively the province of the wealthy few. Specimens sold for literally hundreds of pounds or dollars apiece, largely because they were kept as fur animals, not pets. But times change, as do attitudes. The fur trade has all but ended and chinchillas have been found to make wonderful pets. Although still more expensive than the average small rodent pet, the purchase price of a standard chinchilla has brought them within easier reach of the general pet owner, with any extra expense in the purchase price being offset by the animal's longevity, good nature and minor demands.

History of chinchillas

The ranch chinchilla, *Chinchilla lanigera*, is a member of the rodent family, but more specifically is a member of the sub-order *Hystriocomorpha*, which also includes guinea pigs. The chinchilla's natural habitat is in the Andes mountain range in South America. The ancient Incas were the first to exploit these robust little animals, initially as a food source and then for their luxurious, dense fur. Later, when the Spanish conquistadors overran Peru and the Incan civilization, thousands of chinchillas were captured and exported to Spain between the 16th and 18th centuries. Chinchilla fur, much denser than any other fur found in the world, was highly sought after and priced accordingly. However, the trappers drove the chinchilla to near extinction. Paradoxically, this actually saved the chinchilla, as the bottom dropped out of the fur market and the trappers looked elsewhere for the latest fad.

The Chilean government drew up legislation at the turn of the 20th century to limit the small fur trade in chinchilla fur to specially licensed chinchilla farms. In 1923, the population was deemed to have recovered sufficiently for the government to grant a special licence to Mathias Chapman, an American mining engineer, to allow him to trap a

CHINCHILLAS

limited number of wild chinchillas. Chapman organised a chinchilla trapping expedition and captured 23 specimens, which were duly shipped off to north America. Eleven animals survived the journey – eight males and three females – and these were safely ensconced in Chapman's specially prepared chinchilla ranch in California, where they were housed in purpose-built concrete bunkers.

The animals eventually bred and the first US-born chinchillas were sold for the staggering price of $3,500 (about £1,150) each, a small fortune in the 1920s. In time, several other chinchilla ranches sprang up, many of the would-be breeders lured by the prospect of making a fast buck in the burgeoning fur trade of the mid to late 1920s. Some even banded together in a consortium to buy a pair of chinchillas on a 'stocks and shares' basis, leading to a number of 'Chinchilla cartels'.

The first US-born chinchillas were sold for a staggering price of $3,500, a small fortune in the 1920s

The first fur chinchillas were imported into the UK in 1954, when the price had dropped to a more manageable, but still steep, £250 to £400 a piece. In time, new colours were developed from the original grey, adding to their value.

Over the years, however, the fur trade began to decline and was no longer seen as ethically sound. As a result, a number of clubs began to spring up to cater for people who kept chinchillas purely as pets or for exhibition purposes.

Acquiring a chinchilla

The average adult chinchilla has a rather squat appearance, measuring about 30-35cm (12-14in), with whiskers measuring up to 12.5cm (5in) long with a wiry, bushy tail measuring between 10cm and 12.5cm (4in to 5in) long. Its eyes should be bold and bright and its ears thin, well-set and erect. The adult body weight is between 500g and 600g.

The chinchilla's long whiskers are invaluable in helping it sense objects in the dark, as, in the wild, chinchillas are naturally nocturnal. That said, domestic chinchillas will adapt their

CHINCHILLAS

activity patterns around the lifestyle of their owners and become more diurnal in their habits.

Chinchillas are quite sociable animals and will usually live happily together. A single sex pair, as always, is the ideal choice, preventing unwanted matings while still allowing the animals to have company.

The most striking feature of a chinchilla is, of course, its fur. It should be dense and dry, soft to the touch, not greasy, harsh or patchy. There are over 2,000 individual hairs to every 2.5cm (1in) of the animal's body. As with any healthy animal, a chinchilla should always be alert and interested in its surroundings.

Many larger pet shops sell chinchillas, although it is always better to visit a chinchilla breeder, who will be best able to advise you as to whether a chinchilla is a suitable pet for you. Breeders can be found by contacting your local chinchilla club, which will most likely log its details on the internet. Some breeders advertise via the internet too.

The most striking feature of a chinchillas is its fur, which should be dense, dry and soft to the touch

Housing

One of the most important ways in which a chinchilla differs from its small rodent cousins is that it requires very specialised housing. Special wire construction chinchilla cages are readily available from major suppliers and should be marketed as the only correct home for a chinchilla to live in. Although the all-wire cage may seem rather basic, it has been designed with the needs of the Chinchilla in mind. The mesh gauge should be 2cm x 2cm (0.75in x 0.75in) in width, to prevent the chinchilla's delicate toes from being trapped. A cage suitable for a single animal should measure not less than 60cm x 60cm x 35cm (24in x 24in x 14in) high, whereas a pair should be housed in larger accommodation measuring at least 75cm x 60cm x 35cm (30in x 24in x 14ins) high. The cages should certainly be no higher than these dimensions, for although chinchillas are very agile a fall from a significant height can prove fatal, if not by injury then by bringing on a heart attack through shock.

CHINCHILLAS

Exercise wheels are not required, as these too can induce heart attacks. A piece of clean, white wood may be provided for the chinchilla to exercise its rodent teeth. Branches to climb on and a small shelf to sit on are also appreciated, as chinchillas often feel safer resting above floor level. The cage needs no sawdust or wood shavings, as these will cling to the animal's fur and soil it. Instead, a pull-out tray lined with newspaper is adequate to catch any droppings and urine and may be changed regularly with ease. A hayrack should be placed on one wall of the cage so that the chinchilla can extract as much or as little hay as its wishes to eat, as this provides necessary roughage in the diet.

Some chinchillas will use a wooden nest box, which should be big enough to fit into the cage and allow the chinchillas to sleep inside. Others simply aren't bothered.

ACCESSORIES CHECK LIST

- Proper, purpose-built chinchilla cage
- Hay rack
- Nest-box (optional)
- Strong food bowls
- Water bottle
- Sand bath

Feeding

Feeding is remarkably simple and many new chinchilla owners can be quite worried that their pet's diet may seem boring. However, a great deal of research has been conducted into the ideal diet for chinchillas and specially prepared chinchilla pellets contain all the necessary nutritional requirements, vitamins, proteins and minerals. Rabbit pellets are not a suitable substitute, as these contain other elements which may be harmful to chinchillas. Well-dried, fresh hay, as mentioned above, provides necessary roughage in the diet.

For an occasional treat, a raisin, grape or small piece of apple may be given and will be relished by the chinchilla. Sunflower seeds and peanuts are best avoided, as these are too rich in protein and can adversely affect the chinchilla's coat and skin

General care and maintenance

Chinchillas must be housed indoors at a constant temperature range of 15-20°C (60-70°F). Cool, dry conditions are best, while damp, humid or hot conditions can swiftly lead to illness.

CHINCHILLAS

The most essential item of chinchilla maintenance and good health is the sand bath. Again, the sand is specially marketed, fine sand purely for chinchillas to 'bathe' in. The sand should be placed in a shallow tray – a clean oven tray will suffice – and this should be placed within the cage. The chinchilla will roll happily in the sand for a few minutes, working the sand through the fine hairs of its coat and generally purifying and oxygenating the hairs in this way. When the chinchilla has finished its ablutions, it tends to signify this by defecating in the sand. At this point, the tray should be removed and the sand thrown away. Clean, fresh sand should be used with every sand bath, which may be given up to three times a week, more frequently if the chinchilla's coat looks greasy. But remember, on no account should you ever bath a chinchilla in water!

Special wire construction chinchilla cages are readily available

Chinchillas can be tamed very easily, with a careful 'get to know you' procedure being adopted by the owner. In this way, the chinchilla will quite happily bound out of its open cage door and scuttle all over its owner, often sitting on its owner's shoulder in a very contented and somewhat proprietorial manner. When handling chinchillas, due care must be taken. The best method is grasp the chinchilla firmly by the base of the tail – never the tip – and support its body with your hand under its abdomen. When the chinchilla has become tamer, it may be picked up by placing one hand over its back and midriff, with the other hand again acting as a support. Never hold a chinchilla too high from the floor! Ailments tend to be confined to minor abrasions and dry skin, or typical conditions such as diarrhoea and constipation, most of which are easily treated. If in doubt, take your chinchilla to the vet. Properly cared for, the chinchilla can live a remarkably long life for such a small animal, ranging between 10 and 20 years.

Chinchillas can be tamed very easily, with a careful 'get to know you' procedure

CHINCHILLAS

Breeding

Chinchillas usually reach sexual maturity at six months of age and a pair will mate when the female is in heat. A mixed sex pair that live together will simply get on with things as they desire. However, if you need to introduce a breeding pair to each other, this is best done on neutral territory – eg, in a separate cage to that which they normally live in – so there is no territorial instinct on either animal's part. Mating is seldom observed, usually taking place at night, but the evidence of a successful mating is that the female will display a whitish, rubbery 'plug' on her vent, which will be expelled after she has mated successfully. After this, the male should be removed to his own cage.

The most essential item of chinchilla maintenance and good health is the sand bath

The gestation period is much longer than in other species of rodent, ranging between 111 and 128 days. The female shows signs of pregnancy after about 60 days; obvious symptoms being an enlarged abdomen and swelling of her teats. Some breeders add powdered milk or a calcium supplement to the female's diet at this time to help build her up. If the female does not normally use a nest box, she should welcome one at this stage and this should be kept scrupulously clean. Spread paper towelling on the floor of the cage to prevent the babies from being injured when they are born and also to absorb blood and other birth fluids.

The female usually gives birth to two, sometimes three babies (called kits), although larger litters have been recorded. The kits are born fully formed, with fur and with their eyes and ears open, although they will, of course, need to suckle from the female. Like most rodents, the female will experience post-partum oestrus immediately after the birth and will be receptive to mating – another good reason for the male not being around!

The kits grow quickly and, as soon as their teeth develop, the female understandably feels uncomfortable while suckling them. The kits will start to nibble at food pellets instead. Some breeders recommend adding some calcium supplements to the

CHINCHILLAS

dry food, possibly even baby cereal to help build up the kits' bones and teeth. Very soon, the youngsters will be eating normally and bounding around the cage playing. They may be weaned from their mother at seven to eight weeks and must be split into single sex groups by the time they are four months old, as some chinchillas reach sexual maturity earlier than others! Sexing the kits is easy, as there is a larger gap between the anus and the genitalia in male chinchillas than in females.

Showing and varieties

The standard grey chinchilla is the wild colour and is the most readily available, at the lowest prices. There are, however, close on 40 different colour varieties, all logged and judged at chinchilla shows staged by the various clubs. Among the different varieties are black, beige, white, brown velvet, charcoal and pink white. These are, of course, priced according to rarity.

In the UK, there is a set show season, between September and March, and during this time a number of different graded shows are staged, including special shows purely for novice chinchilla fanciers. Show seasons vary in other countries and are most likely geared towards the cooler months of the year.

As ever, attending a show brings you into contact with other chinchilla lovers and you can gain valuable information about the care and well-being of your chinchillas, as well as the chance to take part in friendly competition.

The standard grey chinchilla is the wild colour and is the most readily available, at the lowest prices

FERRETS

Ferrets are wonderful animals that have a very misplaced reputation. Ask most people what they think of ferrets and you will get the answer: smelly, vicious animals. Anyone who has kept ferrets will know how wrong this image is, they make fantastic pets and, if kept correctly, do not smell and can be extremely loving.

History of ferrets

Ferrets are domesticated animals and have been for many thousands of years. It is believed they are the domesticated form of the European polecat and, given the chance, they will breed with the wild polecat. This has often led to confusion as to whether someone has a polecat or a ferret. Wild polecats and crosses between the two are not easy to handle as they retain the wild characteristics of polecats.

Ferrets come in many colours, including the natural polecat markings, sandy, silver mitts and chocolate-coloured. Most people will always think of the white or albino ferret as the traditional colour.

The ferret's Latin name is *Mustela putorius*. It is part of the *Mustelidae* family which includes weasels, polecats, mink, martens and badgers, to name but a few. The ferret and its relatives are carnivores and all have scent glands.

It is believed that the ferret came to Britain with the Romans, but the first written records of ferrets do not appear until about the 14th century. The name ferret comes from the medieval Latin word *furo* meaning 'thief-like' and that certainly is true of ferrets, because, yes, they will 'steal' things to play with, but they will surely steal your heart once you get to know them!

They were traditionally kept for catching rabbits to eat and for controlling pests such as wild rats and mice, a practice termed 'ferreting'. Although ferreting still takes place today, modern methods have taken over. It is possible for anyone to go ferreting and, if you want to find out more about this, there are lots of clubs that will give you guidance and help.

FERRETS

Ferrets used in this practice are working ferrets, generally kept in hutches outdoors and are very 'mean and keen'.

Ferrets were also kept for their fur, known as fitch, but changing tastes in fashion have almost stopped this industry. This has led to more people finding out what wonderful pets ferrets make, thus most ferrets today are kept in people's homes.

Ferrets make fantastic pets for those who live in small spaces and will happily live in towns and cities. You can have several living together and they can be taken for walks like dogs. Nowadays, most pet shops carry a whole range of ferret cages, accessories and toys.

Acquiring a ferret

There are many places to acquire your ferret, but never purchase one on impulse. The best place to find a good pet ferret is from a pet breeder, although some ferrets from working homes will be just as good, it is a matter of how they are handled and treated.

The ideal age to get your new ferret is eight to ten weeks, when the ferret is old enough to leave its mother and is at the ideal age to learn and adapt to its new owner and home.

Ferrets are also social creatures and should be kept with other ferrets. This will not make them any less friendly towards you, but gives them some added company. If you spend lots of time with them they will treat you just like one of the ferret gang! The main choice to make will be whether to have hobs (males) or jills (females). It is advisable to have both sexes neutered when keeping them as pets, so, as long as you have them neutered before they come into season, you can always have both hobs and jills together!

Because ferrets are seasonal breeders there will be a lot of babies around during the summer months. Occasionally you will find young ferrets in late winter months but this is very rare. A good breeder will be able to show you the parents of your ferrets and where and how their ferrets are kept. Be wary of anyone who wants to meet you away from where the ferrets

Ferrets are social creatures and should be kept with other ferrets

FERRETS

are kept. Qualities to look for are that all the animals are clean and free from diarrhoea or other signs of illness and that they are well-handled animals, not afraid of humans, although you may find some ferrets are not happy with strangers.

Cages should be bright, airy and clean, with clean food bowls and fresh water available. A good breeder will be able to provide you with the date of birth of your ferret along with a feeding guide (and some food to take away with you) and be willing to help if you have any problems.

All of the above will apply to pet shops and rescues centres although they will not be able to show you the ferret's parents. Unfortunately, there are many ferrets who end up in rescue centres every year. It is very worthwhile taking on a rescued ferret, but do be aware if you take on an older animal they may come with their own set of problems.

A good breeder will be able to provide you with the date of birth of your ferret along with a feeding guide

Feeding

Ferrets are carnivores, and need a diet that is very similar to their wild polecat relatives. When keeping any animal as a pet, we owe it to them to provide the best possible diet, which in the case of ferrets would be whole fresh carcasses. Wild ferrets will kill prey animals from mice to rabbits and eat all parts of the animal, including bones. It is possible to feed ferrets whole carcasses and for them still to be perfectly tame pets. A constantly hungry and badly fed ferret is likely to bite, whereas a well fed ferret's behaviour is not determined by its diet and should be docile. A whole carcass diet will provide a ferret with everything it needs nutritionally, but it is not easy to do this for the average pet ferret and often whole carcasses will carry

diseases and parasites. This would also be unpleasant if you kept your ferret in the house.

A constantly hungry and badly fed ferret is likely to bite – be warned!

Thankfully, nowadays there are lots of commercial ferret foods which will provide your ferret with its full nutritional requirements. These foods are usually found in the form of dry

FERRETS

nuggets. However, it is good for your ferret if you can give it some fresh meat at least twice a week as a supplement to its complete food diet. This meat is available in the form of frozen mince available in most pet shops.

You will need to provide your ferret with fresh food every day. There are two schools of thought about whether ferrets should have access to food all day or just given enough for a meal. Ferrets are very restrained in their eating habits and will not usually eat more than they need. Excess food will get hidden by your ferrets, as this is part of its natural behaviour, so do make sure to check the cage every day and remove any uneaten food, otherwise it will go stale and smell.

Avoid cereals and limit tinned cat and dog foods as these can give ferrets loose droppings. Milk can be given occasionally, but too much can also cause loose droppings. Ensure your ferret always has access to fresh clean drinking water, best dispensed from a water bottle. Although ferrets will drink from a bowl they are likely to spill it while playing.

Ferrets like to climb, so you can have tall cages with lots of shelves and different levels

Ferrets will accept treats and, as well as commercial treats that are now available, you can give them a range of table scraps, as long as they are in small quantities, as too many treats mean overweight pets. Different ferrets will have different tastes. However, as many ferret owners will tell you, most ferrets love ice cream.

Daily care

The day-to-day care of ferrets is surprisingly simple, as they are quite undemanding. They do, however, need care and attention every day and the more time you spend with your ferrets the more you will get from them.

Apart from feeding, the main daily chore will be to clean the litter box part of the cage. Thankfully, this is a quick and easy job as ferrets are naturally very clean animals and will always use the same corner of the cage for their toilet. You may not be able to get them to use the corner you want though, as they

FERRETS

will favour one corner that they like over any other. The most important thing to make this an easy job for yourself is to remember that ferrets naturally back up into the corner to go to the toilet. You need to provide a high-backed litter tray to make sure you catch all their waste products and to help make your ferret feel secure. Such litter trays can be bought in most pet shops.

Once a week you will need to clean out the whole cage and replace dirty bedding with fresh. Giving your ferret a quick daily health check will not only give you a chance to get to know your ferret, it will help you spot any problems as soon as they occur.

Housing

The type of cage you choose for your ferrets will depend on where you will be keeping them. You will find there are lots of commercial cages available or you can build your own. The most important thing is that the cage is escape-proof. Simply take a look at the depth of your ferret's head, this is the size of gap your ferret can get through!

If you are keeping your ferrets indoors, choose the largest cage you can fit in your house. Try and choose one that will be easy to clean. Ferrets like to climb, so you can have tall cages with lots of shelves and different levels, tubes, tunnels and hiding-holes to scuttle into. Ferrets also like to play in hammocks and adore soft beds they can hide in.

If you are going to keep your ferrets outside you could choose a rabbit-type hutch, but what would be much nicer, if you have the room, is a ferret court. This is like a shed with an outdoor run attached that the ferrets can use. This is an ideal set up if you have lots of ferrets; make sure to provide lots of beds to hide in. You will have more fun from a ferret court if you can get in and play with your ferrets. Ferret courts are available from specialist suppliers and larger pet stores.

ACCESSORIES CHECK LIST

- Cage – indoor or outdoor
- Bedding – wood-shavings or similar litter for the floor
- Soft comfy bedding for the nest
- Food bowl and food
- Drinking bottle
- Harness and lead
- Toys – hammocks, ropes, balls, tubes to hide in. Even cardboard boxes!

FERRETS

Handling and exercise

Ferrets are very sensitive animals and, when handling, it is important to understand your ferret's natural instincts and why it behaves in certain ways. Albino ferrets with pink eyes have very bad eyesight and will respond to your voice before they see you. When approaching your ferrets make sure you talk to them. Some keepers use a certain noise to let their ferrets know they are coming; this can be jangling keys or a whistle. Whichever noise you choose, make sure it does not sound like a mouse or a rabbit! Ferrets also rely on their sense of smell and can be upset by strong aftershave or perfume. Remember strong smells can make you seem tasty.

All ferrets love to be tickled and each ferret will have their own favourite spot, make sure you take the time to find out your ferret's 'tickle spot'.

When picking up a ferret that knows and trusts you, they should be happy and relaxed, and willing to be held. They will also enjoy being carried around in a pocket or inside your jacket, often snuggling down to sleep.

Ferrets can be trained to walk on a leash, but do use a special harness rather than a collar, as a ferret will easily slip out of a collar. Do get your ferret used to coming when called, although, like cats, this will only be when they choose to do so.

If you do find yourself with a ferret that bites, through being mishandled in a previous home or being frightened, there are various ways of getting them out of the habit. These methods are beyond the scope of this book, but your local ferret club will be able to help you. Don't give up on your ferret – seek help from experts in your area.

There are lots of commercial cages available or you can build your own

Breeding

If you do wish to breed your ferret, please think about this carefully. Again, the best place to start for advice will be your local ferret club. If you do decide you want to breed your ferret, be prepared for up to 17 babies in a litter, although six to nine

FERRETS

is the usual litter size. However, remember that there is a limit to the number of good pet homes for ferrets, so only breed your ferrets if you are prepared to keep any babies that homes can't be found for.

Ferrets are seasonal breeders, with a cycle known as photoperiodic breeding. This basically means that the female comes into heat when the daylight length is long enough and she will remain in heat until she is mated or until the daylight hours shorten. This is important to understand as it can be very harmful for a jill to remain in heat every summer without being mated. It can cause her serious health problems, so always get your jills spayed when they are old enough.

The hobs also become ready for mating during the summer months. This does not pose much risk to their health, although, if left uncastrated, they can become aggressive. This will usually be directed to other hobs, but they have been known to regard male human members of the household as competition too and this can lead to aggressive behaviour.

Your vet will be able to advise you on the best time to neuter your ferret. Please also be sure to consult your vet if you are worried about your pet at any time.

Showing

Ferret shows are a great place to meet other ferret keepers, although showing ferrets is not as serious as showing dogs or cats. You will find that there are lots of other fun events that you can go to with your ferrets, including ferret racing. Ferret racing events are often held at country fairs, so you get lots of members of the public watching and money is usually raised for charity or the local ferret club. Ferrets are placed at the end of long drainpipes laid in rows on the ground, the ferret who is first to come out the other end is the winner. Sounds simple? Not with ferrets around, so you can be sure of a lot of ferret fun!

HEALTH HINTS

- Ferrets are very bad at lowering their body heat, so watch out in the summer for ferrets getting overheated. Make sure if they live outside that they are not in direct sun. If your ferret does get overheated, help it cool down by drenching with cold water and using a fan to provide cooling air, as the lungs are the main means of heat exchange in a ferret.

- Ferrets should be vaccinated against canine distemper, to which they are very susceptible, as well as leptospirosis, especially if you keep dogs or walk your ferrets where lots of dogs also go.

- Ferrets often lose their fur, this can be for several reasons. If you keep your ferrets indoors, this may be caused by central heating causing them to be too hot and uncomfortable, or it could be caused by too much raw egg, which can cause a biotin deficiency. Hormones can also cause hair loss, but if you are unsure about the reason, take your ferret to a vet.

FISH

Keeping fish as pets is a little different to most other animals. You can't cuddle them or take them for a walk, and they won't fetch a ball. They are, however, fascinating animals that can and will interact with their human owners. They are captivating to watch with many different strategies for feeding, breeding and moving. Fish are also very relaxing to watch and studies have shown that watching fish in an aquarium can lower your heart rate and blood pressure.

The healthy fish and getting started

Fish are totally dependent on their environment. This is because their bodies and breathing apparatus (called gills) are in intimate contact with the water in which they live. This water is used by the fish to supply it with oxygen and minerals, chemical signals in the form of smells and pheromones, and even sound in the form of pressure waves. Fish also use water to take away their bodily waste products in the form of ammonia excreted from their gills and solid waste excreted directly into the water.

Because of these things the fish are entirely dependent on the quality of the water that they live in. The ultimate controller of the water quality is the person looking after the fish's aquarium.

To understand how to manage the water quality in an aquarium, it is useful to have some knowledge of the nitrogen cycle. Basically, the one thing that is added to the fish's environment, whether a tropical fish tank, a marine fish tank, a goldfish or Koi pond, is the fish food. This usually comes as a dry food, such as flakes or pellets, and sometimes as frozen foods or live food, such as bloodworms or daphnia. The food should be fed in quantities that the fish will eat very quickly. Under no circumstances should there be any food left uneaten in the tank as this will quickly decompose and cause severe water quality problems.

FISH

When fish eat food, their digestive process immediately starts to take place. This process uses up oxygen that the fish take up from the water through their gills. As stated above, the end products of the fish's digestion and daily metabolism are solid waste, as well as ammonia from the gills. Ammonia is extremely toxic at levels of 0.5 parts per million of water and above. It causes, among other things, mucus clogging of the gills and excess mucus production all over the fish.

The best way of dealing with this problem is by the use of a biological filter. This is a way of passing the aquarium water through a medium with a high surface area, such as open celled foam or ceramic media. On the surface of this biological media live millions of good bacteria that feed on the fish waste. The bacteria first take the ammonia and convert it in to nitrite and then from nitrite into nitrate.

The principles of biological filtration are virtually the same whether you are keeping goldfish in a small tank, a large marine system or even a goldfish or Koi pond

The bacteria that grow first are the kind that convert ammonia into nitrite and these usually appear within one to two weeks. Nitrite is toxic at 0.5–0.75 parts per million and above. This is the pollutant that usually causes the most problems in a new un-matured tank, causing new tank syndrome. The bacteria that make nitrite into nitrate are quite slow to grow taking between 8–12 weeks. The time this takes to happen is called the maturing period. During this period the number of fish kept must be built up slowly and water quality closely monitored. This can be done with a water test kit available from all good aquatic shops.

Nitrate, which is the end product of the breakdown of all organic nutrients put in the tanks, does not readily break down any further and continues to build up in the aquarium, sometimes reaching levels of hundreds of parts per million. Nitrate is less toxic than ammonia and nitrite and, in most aquariums, levels of up to 50 parts per million are fairly safe, although in high concentrations it can affect liver function and blood haemoglobin.

FISH

The best way of getting rid of nitrate is by regular water changes using tap water or water that has been purified using a nitrate resin filter or a reverse osmosis unit. If using tap water, a dechlorinator must be used which is normally a liquid and readily available from most aquatic shops. Regular monitoring of the tank water using a test kit is recommended. If high levels are found, then water changes can be done to try and bring the levels down.

There are also special resins on the market that come in small bags. These can be placed in the filter and are usually recharged using a salt solution. There are three main types of filters on the market:

- The internal power filter, which consists of a container with a sponge biological filter and sometimes an activated carbon chemical filter. (Carbon helps to clarify water-absorbing, toxic pollutants such as phenols and tannins, which can come about from the breakdown of various organic substances.) These filters are placed inside the aquarium and are usually powered by a small water pump forming part of the unit.

- The external power filter. This is a box, usually plastic, which sits outside the tank and is full of media such as biological foam, ceramic media and activated carbon. There is usually space for other media to be used, such as nitrate resin. There is usually a small pump built into the unit and water is taken to and from the tank using plastic tubing.

- Under gravel filters. These consist of a plastic plate on the bottom of the tank over which is placed a layer of gravel 5–8cm deep. The gravel acts as a home for the nitrifying bacteria and traps solid detritus. These filters are usually run by an air pump that sits outside the tank. (Remember to use a non-return valve to stop back-siphoning into the pump). This pumps air down a tube called an uplift, drawing water through the gravel bed. Another way of moving the water through the gravel bed is by using a small water pump called a powerhead.

Goldfish are usually most people's introduction to the art of fish keeping

FISH

Another piece of essential equipment for keeping tropical fish, either freshwater or marine, is a heater. These are small, usually glass, tubes containing a heating element and thermostat, and are normally controlled by an external dial. You will also need a thermometer. There are two main types: glass ones that float inside the tank or a strip type that sticks outside the tank on the glass. If you want to go really hi-tech you can get electronic thermometers that sit outside the tank with a probe in the water to measure the temperature. The principles of biological filtration and the basic processes are virtually the same whether you are keeping goldfish in a small tank, a large marine system or even a goldfish or Koi pond; it is just done on different-sized scales.

Keeping coldwater fish

Coldwater fish can be divided into three main groups:

- Indoor coldwater, including goldfish and the more fancy goldfish, such as black moors, orandas, telescope eyes, Ryukin and lionheads. There are other types of coldwater fish for the indoor aquarium such as White Cloud Mountain minnow, paradise fish, American flag fish, weather loach, various sunbass and coldwater algae eaters.

- Koi – a colour form of the common carp which originated in Japan.

- Other pond fish, including goldfish in various colours and their varieties such as shubunkins, sarassa comets, wakins, golden and blue orfe, tench (both golden and green), grass carp in golden and green, golden minnows and various sturgeon species.

Indoor coldwater fish

Goldfish are usually most people's introduction to the art of fish keeping, quite often through winning the fish at the fairground, although this practice is less common than it was and should really be discouraged on animal welfare grounds. Goldfish and

A red Ryukin goldfish: the Chinese first began the culture of keeping goldfish in 1000AD

FISH

coldwater fish are readily available at most reputable aquarium stores and garden centres with a good aquatic section.

The goldfish is probably the fish with the longest history of any pet fish. The Chinese first began the culture of keeping goldfish during the Sung dynasty (AD 960–1279).

Colour mutations must have been spotted in wild stocks and then captured. Through selective breeding, more and more varieties were developed. The first large shipment to Japan was in 1502 and, since then, the Japanese have developed their own unique varieties such as the Ryukin, named after the Japanese islands of Ryukyu. Goldfish were first exported to Europe in 1611.

Most goldfish varieties were originally bred to be viewed from above – the Chinese used to keep them in large open-topped ceramic bowls – although most people, especially in the West, now keep them in aquariums or garden ponds. The Victorians were very keen on fish keeping and were the inventors of metal-framed glass aquariums and goldfish bowls.

Although most people think of a bowl as a natural home for a goldfish, it is in fact very unsuitable, usually being too small, with a very small surface area to volume of water and no provision for filtration.
In recent years some manufactures have developed larger bowls with fully integrated filtration and lighting systems.

Goldfish were originally bred to be viewed from above – the Chinese kept them in large open-topped ceramic bowls

The fancy varieties of goldfish are more difficult to keep than most tropical fish. This is mainly due to the hundreds of years of inbreeding altering the body shapes and, as a consequence, the change in the shape and configuration of the internal organs. Another factor is that goldfish tend to be larger than most community tropical fish, have a higher demand for oxygen and produce more waste products than tropical fish. The environment of tropical fish is also more stable due to the inclusion of a heater, negating the effects of any temperature swing in the environment.

FISH

Fancy goldfish, with their altered body shapes, are also more prone to balance disorders: the fish lose balance, tend to float upside down and have difficulty in swimming straight. There are three main causes of this:

- Gut problems, either through ingesting air from the water surface when feeding or from constipation, due to the wrong diet or not enough roughage in the diet. This condition can usually be cured by feeding food that sinks and by feeding live or frozen bloodworms, which seem to act as a laxative.

- Swim bladder problem, again often due to the shape of the fish. This can sometimes be alleviated by raising the temperature of the water and by the addition of sea salt at the ratio of one teaspoon to 4.5 litres of aquarium water.

- Bacterial infection of either the gut or swim bladder. There are proprietary treatments specifically designed to treat this problem, available at most aquarium outlets.

Other coldwater species that are commonly kept in indoor aquariums are:

- White Cloud Mountain minnow. A small pretty fish from the mountain streams of China and Hong Kong. These fish are very hardy and will live in quite low temperatures.

- Paradise fish. A small fish of the gourami family, growing to a maximum of 10cm (4in). They can be aggressive, so be careful about which other fish you keep with them.

- American flag fish are another fish that are acceptable in coldwater tanks, but, again, care must be taken, as they can be aggressive towards other fish.

- Weather loach, both brown and golden form, make a good addition to any goldfish aquarium. They are lively and spend time searching out uneaten food in the tank.

- Coldwater sucker fish, also known as Borneo suckers or Chinese butterfly plecos, are a useful fish to have in your goldfish tank as they spend their time eating algae from the surface of the aquarium.

FISH

Breeding goldfish:

Goldfish are egg layers and are easy to breed if kept warm and given a good variety of food. The males vigorously chase the females until they go into the aquatic plants or, if provided, an artificial spawning mop. They then nudge the females and eggs and sperm are released together into the water, where the eggs are fertilised. The eggs immediately become sticky and will adhere to any surface they touch, usually the plants or spawning mop. They will also stick to the aquarium sides and any rocks or décor in the tank.

If you intend to try to rear any of the offspring you will need to remove the spawning media to another well-aerated tank, as the first thing the parent fish do when the eggs have been fertilised is to immediately try and eat them!

The eggs take between 36 to 48 hours to hatch. The baby fish will hang on to the surface where they hatch for a few days, before filling their swim bladders with air and beginning to swim around the tank looking for food. These tiny fish fry need to be fed very small foods such as live, newly hatched, brine shrimp or finely sieved egg yolk. You can also get commercial fry food.

Koi carp are colour mutations of the common carp

Koi

Koi are basically colour mutations of the common carp and, unlike goldfish, the body shape and finnage has to a large extent remained unchanged. It is believed that coloured carp or Koi originated in Niigata, Japan. The rice farmers used carp as a source of protein especially in the winter and it is thought that it was in these carp that the first colour mutations were found. Through selective breeding these fish have produced the many varieties of Koi that we now have.

There seems to be a popular misconception that the Japanese have been breeding coloured Koi for many thousands of years. In fact, the first records of coloured Koi date from the mid-19th century.

FISH

It was not until 1914, when Koi were put into a pond in Tokyo's Ueno Park for the grand Taisho Exhibition, that the Japanese people and the world became aware of these beautiful fish. It was here that they were given the name of Nishikigoi or brocaded carp.

The first recorded commercial import of Koi was in 1966, but it was not until the early 1970s that Koi started to arrive in other countries in any numbers and the first 'Koi only' business did not open in the UK until 1982.

Most people's introduction to Koi is at the garden centre, where they find and purchase some small specimens to put into their small garden pond. Little do they realise that these little fish have the potential to grow to over a metre long and will uproot or eat most of the vegetation that grows in the pond. Many fish keepers proceed to build a succession of larger and technologically more advanced ponds, often spending a lot of money on equipment and fish. The cost of Koi themselves can vary from one figure to five figures for top specimens in the UK.

The one thing that Koi do require is very good water quality with high oxygen levels, and, as they can grow very large very quickly and will consume large volumes of food, the pond needs to be as large as possible with a large, well-designed filter system, including a bottom drain in the pond to take away the solid matter that is produced.

Koi pond and filter construction is a vast and complicated subject and it is best to talk to as many experts as you can and read good quality specialist books so that you can plan the construction properly. Mistakes can be difficult to rectify, as well as expensive. Like all fish keeping, it is better to spend money on the correct equipment, so that tasks such as water changing and filter cleaning are made easier. This will greatly enhance the enjoyment of owning and looking after the fish.

Koi are quite intelligent and often come to recognise the person that feeds them, the container that holds their food and even the time of day when they are feed. If you clap your hands or stamp your feet before feeding they will learn to recognise this

Most people's introduction to Koi and goldfish is at the garden centre, where they find and purchase small specimens for their garden pond

FISH

as a signal that they are to be fed and will eagerly gather around the feeding area. They will, with time, also learn to accept food from your hands. Koi normally live for between 20–30 years, although there have been reports that they can live for up to 100 years!

Koi are still produced in Japan, from where it is thought that the best specimens still come. The earthquake in Niigata in 2004 severely damaged some breeders' fisheries, and it remains to be seen what effect this will have on the trade in Japanese Koi. Israel probably produces the next best quality Koi and in recent years the quality has improved enormously, in some cases rivalling that of the Japanese Koi. Other countries that produce Koi include China, Malaysia, South Africa and Thailand.

There are many Koi societies in the UK and showing these fish has become very popular. Several large shows and lots of small shows are held every year. The fish are judged on a combination of factors including body shape, skin quality, pattern, colour, scalation and deportment, to name but a few. However, unless you seriously want to show your Koi, the best way to choose one is to go for specimens that you personally like and that will give a good overall look and colour balance to your pond.

There are many varieties of Koi. Some of the most common ones are listed below:

- The Kohaku – a white Koi with red markings on its back.
- The Taisho sanke – a white fish with a red and black pattern.
- Utsurimono – a black Koi with red, white or yellow markings.
- Bekko – a white, yellow or red Koi with black markings.
- Goshiki – a white Koi with red markings and a bluish-grey hue throughout the body.
- Asagi – a blue Koi with red markings, usually down the side of the body.

Koi are quite intelligent and often come to recognise the person that feeds them

FISH

- Shusui – a mirror-scaled version of the Asagi.
- Kawarimono – miscellaneous varieties such as Kigoi (yellow Koi), Chagoi (a brown or tea-coloured Koi) and Soragoi (a blue Koi).
- Ogon – a Koi that is just one colour and metallic.

Other pond fish

Other pond fish varieties commonly kept in garden ponds are described below.

Golden Orfe

A long, torpedo-shaped fish growing to around 60cm in length. Look out for new colour variants such as blue orfe and rose orfe. They are mainly surface feeders taking flies and other insects, but will readily take pond pellets. They are very fast swimming fish and can sometimes make other pond inhabitants become a little nervous. They require very high oxygen levels and are usually the first fish to die if the oxygen level drops, whether caused by pump failure or thundery, humid nights when oxygen levels in the air are low. One word of warning with orfe: when they grow to 20cm or more, they are predatory and will catch and eat smaller fish.

Tench

These fish come in two basic varieties: the green tench and the golden tench, although in recent years other colour varieties have been developed. Tench are basically bottom-dwelling fish, which grow up to 60–70cm long. It used to be thought that the slime from a tench could cure diseases in other fish. For this reason it was called the 'doctor fish', but this has no scientific basis and has never been proved.

As green tench live on the bottom of the pond, once they are placed into a pond they are very seldom seen, so the golden tench is probably a better choice if you want to see your fish.

Grass carp

This, again, comes in two basic varieties – the green and the golden grass carp. These fish originate in the Amur river basin

FISH

in China and have the potential to grow up to 2m in length, although they seldom reach this size in the UK. In their native Chinese river, these fish swim upriver to spawn. Their eggs then drift downstream and hatch before they reach the sea. There are no rivers long enough in England to accommodate this and experiments have shown that grass carp cannot breed in the UK. All grass carp available in the UK are artificially propagated using hormone injections.

Grass carp are commonly sold to eat blanket weed in ornamental ponds. (Blanket weed, or cladophora species, is a pest species of green algae that can cause problems in ponds by growing out of control and entangling both fish and plants alike.) They will do this especially when the temperature reaches around 16°C. Unfortunately, they will also eat the other plants in the pond as well, often in preference to the blanket weed! This makes them most suitable for use in Koi ponds which are usually devoid of plants.

Grass carp are very good jumpers so care should be taken to avoid this becoming a problem, especially in the first few weeks after introduction.

Koi carp – Red/White Kohaku

Sturgeon
Another group of fish for the garden pond, which has gained popularity in recent years, is the sturgeon. Sturgeons are 'true' coldwater fish, preferring cool, dark ponds. They are often sold as blanket weed eaters, even though they don't actually eat the blanket weed itself. They will, however, eat the aquatic organisms found in the blanket weed, sometimes becoming trapped and entangled in it.

In the wild, sturgeon eat food that is found on the bottom, such as midge larvae, various shrimps, crayfish, mussels and snails. In captivity, they will readily accept sinking food pellets. However, sturgeon do not do very well in the average garden pond, which is usually too small and shallow to accommodate them. They fare much better in the type of pond used for Koi.

There are three species commonly encountered in aquatic outlets. The first being sterlet or dwarf sturgeon. This is the

FISH

smallest of the three, only growing to about 1m in length; it is a very streamlined fish with a long pointed nose. In recent years an albino form has come on to the market which is very beautiful, but which commands a very high price.

The second species encountered is the diamond sturgeon. This species has the potential to grow much longer, to about 2–3m. It is extremely attractive, having a row of sometimes sparkling scales down its back, and is often compared to a crocodile.

The third species is known by several names including the Russian sturgeon, the long nose sturgeon and the black sturgeon. It is a very dark species, with a long pointed nose and grows up to 3m to 4m in length. Although it is a very impressive fish when large, it is not very ornamental.

When purchasing sturgeon it is much better to go for larger specimens, of 15–18cm or over, because they are not as delicate as smaller fish. It is also important to make sure that they are fat and lively, as it is very difficult to put weight back on a weak sturgeon.

Warning:
Catfish are one type of fish to avoid putting in your pond. There are two species that are occasionally offered for sale: the American channel catfish (available in both blue and gold forms), growing to about 1m in length; and the bullhead catfish, reaching 60–80cm.

Both of these fish are highly predatory and will eat quite large fish when they are fully grown. Do not put these fish into your pond if you value the rest of your pond fish!

Tropical fish

Tropical fish can be divided into roughly six groups. The first and most commonly kept group is the community fish. This describes a very large group of different species that will live together in relative harmony, without bullying, killing or eating each other. These species differ in their hardiness and tend to come from different parts of the world, with vastly different water quality parameters, although most are now captive-bred

Koi carp – Kibekko

FISH

in countries like Singapore, Malaysia, US, Indonesia, Israel and the Czech Republic. Consequently, many of these fish can be classified as domesticated, having been bred under captive conditions for many hundreds of generations.

Tropical fish keeping first started on a commercial scale in the mid 1950s. But it was not until the invention of plastic bags in which to pack the fish and polystyrene boxes to keep them warm, together with the advent of cheap air travel in the 1960s, that tropical fish keeping really started to take off as a hobby.

Keeping tropical fish has never been easier. The modern technology available includes low maintenance filtration, digital heaters, automatic feeders and integrated all-in-one aquarium systems.

When an aquarium is first set up, it is usually advisable to leave it running for about one week without fish. This gives time for the heater to settle down and any dissolved gas to come out of the water. It also gives the maturing process time to start with a little help from a proprietary maturing agent available from any aquatic outlet. After this first week you can start adding a few fish. It is best to add a very few at a time, approximately six small fish for a 70-litre aquarium. The hardiest fish to use are species such as the zebra danios, leopard danios, White Cloud Mountain minnow or x-ray tetras.

Community fish is a very large group of different species that will live together in relative harmony

If these fish are thriving after about a week, then the stock can gradually be built up, taking care to monitor the water quality with test kits and bearing in mind that an aquarium can take approximately 8 to 12 weeks to mature. One of the most common mistakes is to stock a new tank too quickly; the other mistake is to feed the fish too much food. Both result in a deterioration in water quality.

Live-bearers

The most familiar group of fish are the live-bearers. These include species such as the guppy, platys, mollies and swordtails.

FISH

Most people will think of the guppy when they think of tropical fish. These fish have been bred in captivity for many years and now come in a large variety of size and colour, including metallic colours. There are also variations in tail shape such as the lyretail, pintail and swordtail.

Guppy

Traditionally, the male guppy has always been the more colourful, but females are now being bred with more colour in the tails. Guppies grow to around 5cm in length. Most male guppies have a slim body and a large fan-shaped tail. They also have their anal fins modified into a gonopodium, which is used to internally fertilise the female. Female guppies are usually brown-bodied with a much smaller tail than the male. They also have a broad, rounded, anal fin and a dark brood pouch is visible in the abdomen. They are normally fatter than the males and, if they are kept in the presence of males, are usually in a constant state of pregnancy.

Guppies were always thought of as extremely hardy fish and were quite often used as the first fish to mature a new aquarium

Guppies are very easy to breed, but the fry are so small they are usually eaten unless a breeding trap is used. Breeding traps confine the female till she gives birth and the fry are separated from both the female and the rest of the tank. Guppies – like all live-bearers – give birth to fully formed young which require feeding with fry food. Because they have skipped the vulnerable egg stage, there are far fewer live-bearer babies than egg-layer babies, but this gives them the advantage of being bigger and more developed.

Guppies were always thought of as extremely hardy fish and were quite often used as the first fish to mature a new aquarium. Unfortunately, this is no longer the case and they are now rather delicate, possibly through inbreeding and various disease problems. Careful choosing of tank mates is also needed, as their long tails are vulnerable to attack from other fish such as tetras and Siamese fighting fish.

Platys

The next most readily available fish is the platy and most aquarium shops will stock a wide variety of colours. The most

FISH

common types you will see are red platy, red wagtail (red, with black markings on half the body and tail), sunset platys (yellow, with the colouring changing to red on the back half of the body), the black platy, the blue platy, the rainbow platy and the spotted platy. There are many more available, with more varieties being developed all the time.

On the whole, platys are very hardy fish, making them the ideal candidates for stocking a new aquarium. They breed readily and the babies are relatively large, making them quite a good fish to start breeding with. The sexes are fairly similar, but, as with all live-bearers, the males have a gonopodium and the females have a broad anal fin and a deep, rounded abdomen. Platys can grow to around 6–7cm in length.

Swordtails

A very similar species, which is also very popular, is the swordtail. It is a large fish reaching a length of 10–12cm, with a longer body and gets its name from the sword-like projection that the male swordtail grows on his tail when mature. Sometimes this 'sword' can be up to 75% of the body length and can look very stunning. Everything else about swordtails is very similar to the platys, including varieties and breeding.

Mollies

Next are the mollies. The most common types are the black molly, the silver molly and the dalmatian molly. As well as all the other colour types available, there are also different fin types such as lyretail and fantail. The most delicate of the mollies is the black molly which is prone to white mucus on the body and can benefit from a small amount of sea salt added to the aquarium water, which helps this problem.

The breeding of mollies is much the same as with the other live-bearers. One notable difference is the size of the babies, which are much larger in comparison to their parents. Sexing the males is easy as they have a very large dorsal fin, as well as the gonopodium.

Pearl gourami (lace) and lyre tail mollie fish

FISH

There is another species of molly, the sailfin molly. These are much larger than normal and the males have a wonderfully large dorsal fin. They grow up to 12–15cm.

The mouth parts of all mollies are built for rasping algae and plant materials. Bearing this in mind, as well as feeding normal flake food, it is a good idea to use a flake with a high proportion of vegetable matter.

Tetras

The next and possibly the largest group of aquarium fish is the tetras. It is a huge group so we will only be able to deal with the most popular species. The neon tetra has to be the most popular fish kept in aquariums today. It is a small fish, a maximum of 3cm, with an almost fluorescent blue stripe running from head to tail with a band of red running half way down the body. They are hardy little fish, which form schools of usually six or more. They are content to eat flake food and will quite often breed, but, being egg-scatterers, the fry seldom survive past hatching before being eaten.

A similar species to the neon tetra is the cardinal tetra. This is a much more spectacular fish, attaining a larger length of 4–5cm. The body is deeper and the red stripe runs the whole length of the body. Its habits are similar to the neon tetra but the cardinal is more delicate and will sometimes 'faint' when caught and placed in a bag to be transported home.

Other readily available tetras include the black neons, serpae tetras, bleeding heart tetras, lemon tetras, pristella or x-ray tetras, Buenos Aires tetras, glowlight tetras, head-and-taillight tetras, black widows, rummy-nose tetras and Congo tetras.

All tetras have very similar living and breeding requirements. Some are known to be fin nippers of fish with long fins. The worst offenders are red eye tetras, serpae tetras and black widows. On the whole they are a peaceful group of fish, fitting in with most other types of fish.

Barbs

Barbs are, on the whole, a little larger than most tetras, some reaching lengths of up to 30–40cm for species such as the

Gouramis are a popular breed of fish

tinfoil barb. Barbs are all egg-scatterers and so, although they will breed in a community tank, the eggs and fry are usually eaten. In east Asia, they are often dyed or injected with colour, but these fish are seldom imported and should be avoided.

Below is a selection of barbs, but look out for all the other interesting species of barb readily available in the shops:

- The most commonly encountered barb is probably the tiger barb, which grows to about 7–8cm. Tiger barbs come in various colours such as green, golden and blushing. Tiger barbs are shoaling fish, as are most barbs, and they tend to cause less chaos in the aquarium if kept in numbers of six or more. They are known fin nippers and should not be kept with fish such as guppies and Siamese fighting fish.

- Cherry barbs are a good colourful addition to any community tank, the males being a dark cherry red colour. They don't grow much over 4–5cm and are usually peaceful, even with long-finned fish, which is unusual for barbs.

- Checkered barbs, which, when larger, develop a mottling of blue, black and orange. They grow to about 3–4cm, with a temperament typical of barbs.

- Golden barbs are gold skinned with a dark line running from head to tail. The neon varieties with sparkling scales on the upper body are very popular. They grow to about 7–8cm.

- Rosy barbs come in several varieties, but the most popular are the neon rosy barb and the long fin rosy barb. It is the male fish that is the most colourful ranging from a deep ruby red to a light metallic orange. Rosy barbs are usually sold in pairs and have a very industrious nature, seldom resting.

Danios

Danios are another good addition to any community tank and are very good for a new tank as they are hardy and peaceful. The zebra, leopard and pearl danios are all very similar in size and habit, reaching a length of about 5–6cm. They are very lively shoaling fish, which use the whole of the aquarium and are fairly peaceful; they also come in long finned and golden

FISH

versions. The other danio you will come across is the giant danio which grows to about 10–12cm. Again, it is a shoaling fish, but do be careful what you keep with them because of their size.

Gouramis

Gouramis are a very popular group of fish, many of the species being quite large. Some fish in this family breed by blowing a bubble nest at the water's surface into which the eggs are laid; the parents then guard this.

The giant, or osphronemus, gourami reaches a length of 60–70cm, normally much too large for most home aquariums.

Blue or opaline gouramis, three-spot gouramis and yellow gouramis are all similar in size and shape, all reaching a maximum of around 15cm. They are quite boisterous and can be territorial and sometimes aggressive to smaller tank mates. They readily accept flake food as their main diet, but will also enjoy live foods.

Angelfish are predatory, especially when large, and this can sometimes cause problems in a community tank

The pearl gourami is probably the most attractive of the large gouramis attaining a length of 15cm. This species is usually very peaceful, almost to the point of being shy, otherwise its habits are very similar to the other gouramis.

The kissing gourami is another potentially large fish reaching about 30cm and becoming aggressive when larger. The dwarf gourami is a good and popular choice for a community aquarium only reaching a size of 6cm. Gourami are available in a wide range of colours including neon varieties. The females tend to be rather dull compared to the males.

There are numerous other species of gouramis including snakeskin, pygmy, thicklip and silver.

Angelfish

Freshwater angelfish have always been popular and deservedly so, with their unusual shape, wide variety of colours and patterns, and bold habits. Angelfish will grow to about 15cm and will thrive on flake food. They usually breed by laying eggs on a flat vertical surface such as a piece of slate or an Amazon

sword plant leaf. They are very protective of their territory around the nest and can become a problem for other tank inhabitants.

Angelfish are predatory, especially when large, and this can cause problems in a community tank. This problem can usually be surmounted by stocking small angelfish and letting them grow up with the other fish.

Catfish

There are thousands of species of catfish (so called because they have whiskers or barbells) and they make an interesting addition to the tank. The most common and popular are the corydoras species. These fish are originally from the Amazon basin in South America and range in size from about 1cm, for corydoras pygmaeus, right up to 10cm, for the brochus species. These fish usually spend most of their time on the bottom of the aquarium feeding on particles of food. Because of this, it is a good idea to use sinking pellet food to make sure that they do not starve.

The freshwater angelfish has always been popular as a pet with its unusual shape and wide variety of colours and patterns

The three most common species are the bronze, albino and peppered cory. They breed by laying eggs on a hard surface such as a rock or the aquarium glass. It is important that the substrate on the tank bottom does not have sharp edges, as these can damage the barbells on the catfish's mouth.

The loricarids are another useful and interesting group of catfish containing hundreds of species. The common pleco is probably the most recognised species and is often sold as an algae eater to keep the sides of the aquarium clean. This it does very well, but it has one drawback: it will reach a size of 60cm or more and very quickly. A much more suitable species is the ancistrus, a very industrious little fish reaching a maximum size of 10–12cm. It is now available as golden and long-finned forms. One problem commonly encountered with them is when they have eaten all the natural algae in the tank they can starve to death. To avoid this, make sure you feed them algae wafers about three times a week.

There are a myriad of catfish available in all different shapes, sizes and colours. It is worth searching round your local aquatic shops for interesting catfish for your tank.

FISH

Other tropical fish

Some people try to classify tropical fish as top, middle and bottom swimmers. This is only vaguely true, as most fish will search out food wherever it is to be found. There are exceptions to this rule and they are the butterflyfish, the hatchetfish and the halfbeak.

The freshwater butterflyfish is a strange-looking fish, almost resembling a half-rotten leaf. It grows to about 10cm and will readily take flake food. It has a very large mouth and will eat small fish.

There are about four or five species of hatchetfish that regularly turn up in the aquatic trade. Most of them reach a size of 4–5cm, are very good community fish and will feed on flake food.

The halfbeak is also a strange fish, reaching a length of around 7–8cm. It is elongated and thin and the lower jaw is longer than the top one. Halfbeaks are live-bearers, so with care can be bred and, even though they look difficult to feed, they will accept flake food.

The silver shark is a fish you will find in most aquatic shops, and is a very popular addition to any tank. Silver sharks, which are no relation of true, sea-swimming sharks, have the potential to reach a size of 20–25cm. They prefer to live in small groups and are very peaceful, even leaving the smallest of fish alone despite their name! Diet is, again, flake with pellets for larger specimens.

A different genus, but with the same common name of shark is another group of fish commonly found for sale, namely the labeo species. They are not related to the sharks you find in the sea, although they were given the name from the resemblance their body shape has to the sea-dwelling sharks. Species include the red-tailed black shark, red fin shark or rainbow shark, and the black shark.

The red-tailed black and the red-finned shark reach a size of 18–20cm, while the black shark reaches a length of around 30cm. All three species are territorial and only one can be kept in a tank. Any more than this and they will fight to the death.

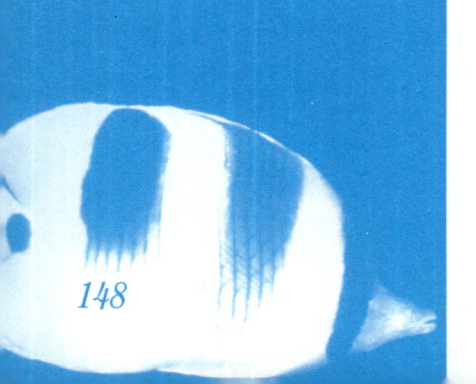

The marine butterfly fish feeds exclusively on coral polyps

FISH

As they grow they can sometime become aggressive towards their tank mates and kill them.

The botias and loaches are interesting, and numerous, groups of fish. Probably the most recognisable fish are the sucking loach, also known as the algae eater, and the clown loach.

The sucking loach comes from fast-flowing hill streams in south-east Asia and can grow up to 20–30cm. It is normally sold as an algae eater and comes in the normal colour of brown, a gold form and a mottled form. It is a very fast fish and can cause trouble as it grows, due to it trying to eat the mucus from the scales of larger slower fish. Although it will tolerate much cooler temperatures than most tropicals, and can live in a coldwater tank, it should not be housed with goldfish as it will attack them to eat the mucus from them.

Of all the loaches the clown loach is undoubtedly the most popular. It is a striking yellow with black stripes and red or orange fins. The clown loach has the potential to reach 25–30cm, but in an aquarium environment usually only reaches 15–18cm. The name, clown loach, comes from its habit of doing strange things such as lying on its side on the bottom of the tank. It loves to eat snails making it very useful in any tank that has been overrun by snails.

The silver shark is a fish you will find in most aquatic shops and is very popular

Clown loaches like to be kept in small groups and are susceptible to white spot until established. You will find many more species of botias and loaches, most of which will make good tank inhabitants.

There are many more species of community fish to be found in aquarium shops, too numerous to cover in this book. New species and colour varieties are appearing all the time, making fish keeping a fascinating hobby with always something new to see.

Non-community fish

There are other types of tropical aquarium fish on the market that require different conditions to a normal community aquarium.

FISH

The family of Cichilidae includes about 2000 species, which range in size from 3cm to about 75cm. Cichlids like to dig in the substrate and this makes any attempt to use an under-gravel filter useless. They will eat virtually anything and there are numerous commercial foods especially for cichlids.

They have various breeding strategies, the most interesting being mouth brooding in the pseudotropheus species. This is where the female lays the eggs and takes them in her mouth; she then nibbles at the egg spots on the male, who fertilises the eggs while they are in the female's mouth.

The female carries the eggs till they hatch and then carries the fry in her mouth till the fry are too big to stay in her mouth, at which point she releases them. By this time, the fry are fully formed and can be quite large – up to 1.5cm – and they instinctively head for cover between the rocks.

Malawi cichlids are very territorial and can be aggressive in confined spaces

The closest you can be to having a marine tank without all the expense is the African rift lake cichlids. They are extremely colourful, coming in lots of different colours and patterns, ranging from electric blue to red and black. These fish come from the various rift lakes of Africa and many are thought to be descended from saltwater fish, as the rift lakes were thought to be connected to the sea many millions of years ago.

The two most popular lakes from which the fish come are Lake Malawi and Lake Tanganyika. From these, Lake Malawi fish are the most widely kept. The African rift lakes have a high pH, about 8, and a high water hardness. This makes keeping them easy, as, in most areas, this is the same pH as tap water.

In most areas, the lakes are very rocky and often have lots of boulders on the bottom. It is important to recreate this in the aquarium with lots of rocks, to provide crevices and holes for the fish to hide in.

Malawi cichlids are very territorial and in the confined space of the aquarium this can manifest itself as aggression. This is the main drawback of keeping these fascinating fish. One way of combatting this is to have a higher stocking density than normal. The way this works is by spreading the aggression throughout the tank, stopping the stronger fish establishing a large territory which they would try and defend.

These cichlids can grow quite large, on average between 10–15cm and an aquarium with a good number of these fish will require a very good filtration system, usually with an external power filter.

The cichlids from Lake Tanganyika are often not as colourful but do exhibit a wonderful range of patterns, body shapes and habits. They tend not to be quite as aggressive as the Malawi cichlids and some species can be mixed into a Malawi set-up, although most fish keepers prefer to keep the two types separate.

Cichlids are notoriously harsh on plant life, but there are two plants that seem to survive their attentions quite well – these are java fern (microsorium) and the giant vallis.

There are several hundred different species in both lakes; the best place to see them and get an idea of the choices is at a well-stocked aquarium shop.

Other types of cichlid are the South and Central American cichlid species, such as the sevrum, oscars and the dwarf cichlids. A lot of these fish come from Amazonian regions and need water of a fairly low pH (6.5–7.5). Some grow large, such as the oscar, and require a very large tank to house them. Again some species can be aggressive, so care should be taken when choosing tank mates.

The dwarf cichlids, such as the ram and the cockatoo cichlid, can be very colourful. Moreover, with due care, they can be kept in a community aquarium.

Another species of non-community fish from the cichlid family are the discus. They are flat and round, like a discus used in sports, and come in many colour varieties, some truly spectacular, with the very best specimens fetching large sums of money. They are not fish that like to be surrounded by huge numbers of small fish, although they will tolerate small numbers of cardinals and corydoras catfish.

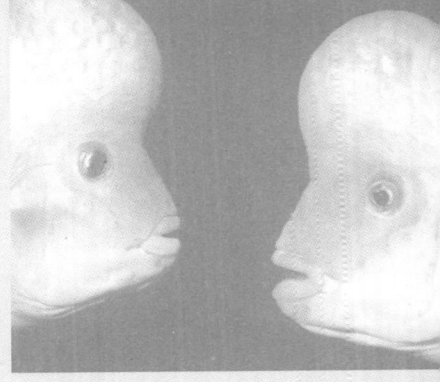

A pair of midas cichlid, found in the large rivers of Central America

FISH

Discus originate from the Amazon and wild-caught discus are still available. The majority of discus offered for sale are captive-bred in countries like Thailand, Malaysia, Indonesia, Germany and the Czech Republic. Discus require very good water quality and a high water temperature of approximately 30°C and soft acid water with a pH of 6.5. They will feed on dry granulated food but seem to prefer frozen foods. These are commercially available and are a mixture of frozen beef heart, bloodworms and other ingredients.

Discus breed on a vertical surface such as slate bog wood or the side of the tank. There are also commercially available ceramic cones for the serious breeder to provide for the discus to lay eggs on.

Discus parents are very attentive to the eggs and fry and have a very unusual way of rearing the fry. The female secretes extra mucus on her flanks and the fry feed on this until they are fairly large.

Tank busters

If you have room for an extra large aquarium, you may like to consider keeping one of the group of fish known as the tank busters. These are a miscellaneous collection of fish that grow very big, and require lots of tank space and very good filtration. These fish are often very intelligent and can become pets with individual personalities. Species include the arrowanas, lungfish and many species of catfish such as the redtail and the shovelnose catfishes.

If you fancy a different type of tank you could always try a brackish water tank. Brackish water fish make an interesting change; the fish come from estuaries and mangrove swamps. There are not many species in this group, but include the monos or sea angels, both similar in appearance and habits. Look out for silver fish with quite deep bodies. Scats are a cream fish with dark spots on the body and can grow to 28–30cm. There are three species of scats.

Archerfish are interesting as they have the ability to shoot water from their mouths. This is used in the wild to shoot at insects from overhanging foliage, which they then eat when they fall into the water.

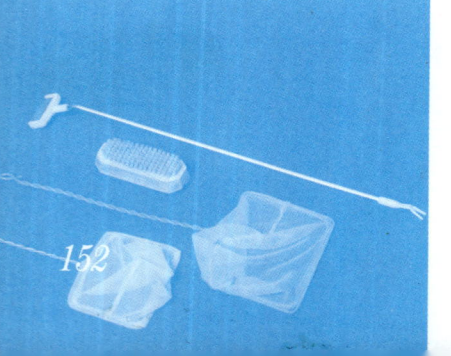

It is important to have the right equipment when keeping fish, such as nets and algae scrappers

FISH

Pufferfish are a very strange group of fish, but because of their endearing smiling faces they are very popular as a pet species. There are three species regularly available, but the most commonly encountered are the green spotted and the figure of eight pufferfish. Both can grow up to 15cm in length and are fed on meaty frozen foods. They can be aggressive and are well-know tail nippers.

Some other brackish water fish are some molly species, mudskippers, moray eels and chromides.

Marine fish

Marine fish keeping is really the pinnacle of aquatics. It is the most difficult and the most expensive, but is also the most rewarding. Marine fish keeping brings into your home a fascinating slice of the tropical coral reef. By their very nature they come from the world's oceans, mostly from areas where there are coral reefs, normally south-east Asia, the Philippines, Malaysia, Sri Lanka and the Red Sea.

Before the advent of the plastic bag and cheap air travel, it was virtually impossible to transport marine fish any distance, so marines were unknown as aquarium species until the mid-1950s and early 1960s, and were far too expensive for most people until the 1970s.

The main problem with marine animals is that their environment is usually very stable, with water parameters such as pH, ammonia, nitrite, nitrate, phosphate, calcium levels, temperature and lighting levels being very constant. They come from extremely complex ecosystems that have taken millions of years to evolve. Thus, they are very intolerant to any environmental change both on the reefs and in an aquarium.

This is one reason why the world's coral reefs seem to be in decline and are threatened with such things as global warming, El Niño (an unusually warm water current), siltation, pH changes due to CO_2 emissions and over-exploitation, both through fishing pressure and the global tourism industry. It is for these reasons that the marine aquarium keeper should do

FISH

their utmost to ensure the well-being and possible propagation of the animals in their care.

Keeping marine fish

Marine fish keeping is an enormously complex subject and so we will only deal with the basics here. The main difference between freshwater and marine aquariums is the salt content of the water. This is usually measured as specific gravity (a direct comparison with pure fresh water), but can also be measured in salinity (parts per thousand), conductivity, and the way the water bends light (refractometry).

The specific gravity of the marine aquarium is usually kept at between 1.019 and 1.022. You would use a hydrometer to measure this, usually with a dip and read type, where you fill the hydrometer with the water to be tested and a small float indicates the specific gravity on a scale.

Before planning a marine set-up consider whether you want a 'fish only' system

Before setting up a marine aquarium, it should be realised that the larger the aquarium, the more stable the environment will be and the easier it will be to keep. It would be very difficult to maintain a marine aquarium of anything under 120 litres for any length of time. This is one time when the more money spent on decent, well thought out equipment, the easier it will be to keep.

One of the main considerations before planning a marine set-up is whether you want a 'fish only' system or whether you want a reef tank which tries to emulate a miniature tropical reef ecosystem, with living rock, corals, anemones, sponges and all the other interesting invertebrates found on the reef. With this sort of set-up you can incorporate fish species that live in harmony and do not attack the other inhabitants.

Once this has been decided, the hardware can be put together. The basic minimum for a fish only system is a good filtration system, consisting of at least an external power filter, with good biological and chemical filtration, and a good quality protein skimmer. You could also go for a system with a sump where all

FISH

the equipment is housed under the tank in another glass tank. This adds the ability to have a dentrifaction unit, automatic top up system, calcium reactor, automatic feeding and trace elements dosing. The protein skimmer could also be added in the sump instead of in the tank. The rest of the equipment is the same as for a tropical tank (a heater and lighting), although you can get much stronger lighting for marine tanks, as they are often deeper than freshwater.

The tank should be kept at a temperature of 26–28°C. Another useful piece of equipment for a fish only system is an ultra violet (UV) sterilisation unit, which shines very strong UV rays through the water as it is pumped through the unit. The UV rays destroy the DNA of anything living that passes through the unit and so killing it. In this way it kills harmful bacteria and parasites that are free-swimming in the water.

Marine fish do from time to time succumb to various diseases: the most common are protozoan diseases, such as white spot; bacterial diseases, such as lateral line diseases; and occasionally crustacean infections, such as sea lice. These can all be treated using a combination of copper-based treatments, fresh water dips and bactericides.

Most marine fish prefer to feed on things they would normally find in their natural environment, such as cockles, mussels, mysid shrimps, krill, brine shrimps, shrimps, cyclops or plankton. These are all readily available frozen in single food types or in mixes, and specialised foods for those fish that only feed on such things as marine sponges.

Breeding marine fish requires laboratory type conditions and although some species like clown fish are quite simple to spawn they are a real challenge to rear. The reason for this is that most marine fish fry are pelagic and become part of the plankton in the sea, feeding on other planktonic organisms. This is very difficult to recreate in the aquarium, requiring specially designed tanks and complicated processes of algal, rotifer and plankton culture just to provide the fry with food. Thankfully, there are dedicated breeders out there who are developing the skills needed to breed more and more species of

Marine fish keeping brings into your home a fascinating slice of the tropical coral reef

155

FISH

marine fish commercially, making them more readily available in the shops.

Reef aquariums are a little bit more complicated and there are many ways of filtering them, ranging from algal filters, living mud filters and even relying on living rock and deep coral sand beds to filter the tank.

Invertebrates require more in the way of water currents as most come from the upper levels of the coral reefs. The other main difference is the lighting. Many corals have symbiotic algae that actually use light and the waste products from their hosts to produce food in the form of simple sugars. The host polyps or anemones then use this as food; because of this, the level and quality of light that they receive is very important and specialised lighting is required. This can take the form of the traditional fluorescent bulbs – around four bulbs would be necessary for the average invert tank – and this should include some tubes emitting light in the UV spectrum which the zoolanthe need to synthesise. These UV bulbs are commonly referred to as actinic bulbs.

The other way of lighting the invertebrate aquarium is to use metal halide lighting, using very high intensity bulbs that closely mimic sunlight. There are two main drawbacks to this system, firstly both the unit and the bulbs are very expensive and they give out a lot of heat. This can overheat the aquarium and become life-threatening to the inhabitants. One way round this is to use a commercially produced chiller unit but again they are not cheap.

Undulatus trigger fish – a popular marine fish

The main base of a reef tank is the living rock, a porous rock made up from a combination of old dead coral skeletons and encrustation of calcareous algae. It also contains all sorts of marine life such as shrimps, crabs and various polyps.

All marine organisms are very intolerant of high levels of nitrates in their water as in natural sea water there is virtually no nitrate. Therefore, careful management is required to avoid the excessive build up of this pollutant.

FISH

Livestock for reef tanks

Livestock available for inclusion in a reef tank are various hard corals including gonipora, acropora species and various bubble corals, to name but a few.

The hard corals are probably the most difficult to keep and grow but are well worth the effort. The other group of coral are the soft corals. These are a little easier to keep than the hard corals and are available in a wide range of species including the mushroom corals or sacrophytons. These come in a wide range of shapes and sizes and polyp forms, even differing in the colour and length of their polyps. Other types include the prickly soft corals again with a wide range of different species and forms, some very pretty with pinks, oranges and reds.

Various zenia species are available, again some are very colourful with brightly coloured polyp centres. Anenomes make good inhabitants of the invert aquaria. They have no skeletons and some can grow quite large. They also provide good homes for the various anenome fish that are available. Most require the provision of ultraviolet lighting. Sponges are another type of invert, the most common ones are the blue sponge from southeast Asia and the red tree sponge from the Caribbean area.

Polyps are individual animals that live on the surface of rocks and other marine objects. They are usually colonial and often give the appearance of corals. There are two main types one is the button polyp, available in a wide range of colours from red to bright luminous green. The other is the mushroom polyp – again colonial – and they come in a range of colours.

Worm species are also available mostly with decorative fan-shaped heads. These include the soft fan worms and the hard-shelled coco worms – all normally associated with a species of hard coral.

The other main group of commonly kept marine life is the crustaceans. The main interest are the various shrimp species.

FISH

There are three main types found in the shops:

- The cleaner shrimp. A small shrimp with red and white stripes down its back. This shrimp as its name suggests will clean parasites from the gills of the other fish who will often queue up for the service.

- The blood shrimp, which is red with small white markings.

- The stenopus is a delicate looking shrimp with red and white banding although you can only keep one to a tank as they are liable to fight.

Hermit crabs can be quite useful as scavengers and come in different sizes, although it is best to avoid the largest as they can attack the other tank mates and dislodge inverts such as corals within the tank.

Other inverts you can put in the tank include: sea apples, sea cucumbers, sea urchins and starfish.

Hermit crabs can be quite useful as scavengers and come in different sizes

In recent years the practice of fraging inverts has become more popular. This is a method of propagating both hard and soft corals. Cuttings are taken rather like the practice of taking cuttings from a garden plant. These small fragments are normally glued to a small piece of rock to provide stability. Coral farms have been set up both in the UK and abroad, and, in years to come, more and more farmed corals will become available as wild-caught specimens become harder to get.

Species of marine fish

Below are just some of the huge number of species available.

Angelfish

Marine angelfish can be divided up into a number of types:

- Dwarf angels, such as the flame angel, the bicolour and the coral beauty, are mostly safe to live with invertebrates and adapt readily to captivity.

- The larger angels, such as the emperor angel, french angel and king angel, grow to around 30cm in length. Most of these

FISH

are not invert friendly. The juvenile fish are very colourful, but change into duller colours as they get older.

Angels are usually very easy to feed and make good aquarium inhabitants.

Butterflyfish
Although the marine butterflyfish are related to angels, they are a little bit more delicate and in general do not reach such a large size. Most are not suitable for invert tanks and some feed exclusively on coral polyps, which makes them almost impossible to keep for any length of time.

Pufferfish
These are definitely not invert-friendly, but are great characters, becoming tame and hand feeding on meaty foods such as prawns, cockles and mussels. It is a good idea to give them whole cockles in their shells to keep their beaks from over-growing.

Tangs
Most tangs are invert-friendly, but will eat algae, which in the wild forms part of their diet. The most popular tangs are the yellow tang and the regal tang, which is a blue colour.

Clownfish
These are probably the most recognised of all marine fish, mainly for their relationship with sea anemones. Most are ideal for invert tanks but some species, such as the maroon clown, can be territorial.

Damselfish
Damselfish are probably the hardiest of the marine fish. They reach only a small size and come in a wide range of colours. Most are invert-friendly, although some can be aggressive especially as they reach maturity.

Gobies and blennies
These are usually small, bottom-dwelling fish. The most commonly kept is the mandarin fish, which can be difficult to feed and usually does better in an invert tank, where it can find food in the form of small shrimps and copiopods. Some gobies perform a useful service in the aquarium such as keeping the sand clean by constantly sifting through it.

Clown/anemone fish – ideal for invert tanks

FISH

Lionfish
These fish are very unusual, having large finnage, and are very majestic swimmers. They range in size from 12–15cm right up to 35–40cm. They are predatory so must not be housed with anything they can fit in their mouths. One word of warning is that their dorsal or top spines are extremely venomous, often resulting in a trip to hospital if you are unlucky enough to get stung.

Trigger fish
These unusually large and robust fish feed on all types of inverts, especially shrimps and crabs. They have large beaks and can sometimes be aggressive towards their tank mates. They are full of character and can make very good pet fish.

Wrasses
There are many species of wrasses, some very colourful, but you have to be careful as they are not all invert-friendly. They can grow quite large. The most recognised wrasse is the cleaner wrasse, a small blue fish that, like the cleaner shrimp, feeds on the external parasites found on fish.

A rewarding hobby

Fish keeping is a great hobby that can be very rewarding but can also be frustrating if things do not go right. Just remember never to rush things: whether stocking the tank or pond or keeping an eye on the water quality, you must be conscious of the day-to-day maintenance of the systems involved in the upkeep of your chosen type of fish. Even when doing this, unexplained things can still happen both good and bad, but that is the nature of fish keeping. It is only through trial and error that many techniques and the secrets of the aquatic worlds have been learned.

A community tank consists of several species that can live peacefully together

FISH

SETTING UP PROBLEMS

Common problems encountered when setting up freshwater tank systems usually have one of two causes:

- **Water quality:** More common in the first few months of a new set-up and best avoided by regular monitoring of water quality using a test kit. Most common mistakes are over-feeding of the fish. Fish are natural scavengers and in the wild are looking for food all the time, although they only come across it occasionally. They carry this behaviour on in captivity and this makes them look as though they are in a permanent state of hunger. This makes it very easy to feed them continually, eventually polluting the water. Most tropical and coldwater fish require feeding only once per day, marine fish possibly a little more frequently and then only in very small amounts.

The other cause of poor water quality is stocking a new tank too quickly, not allowing time for the bacteria to grow to cope with the waste being produced.

- **Diseases:** Quite a lot of the disease problems encountered are caused by water quality problems. If you have poor water quality it can be stressful for the fish, lowering their immune systems; this allows parasites and bacteria, which usually live on the fish without causing a problem, to start adversely affecting the fish.

Another very common cause of disease effecting the fish is when already diseased, stressed or weakened fish are introduced to your healthy stock. There are two main ways to combat this. The first is to be very careful where you purchase your fish, ensuring that you choose a reputable dealer who knows what they are doing and are very conscientious about the husbandry of their stock and disease control. The second is to separately quarantine the newly-acquired stock for a few weeks prior to introducing them into your main system. Although if you just have one small tank you will not be able to do this, it is especially important if you have rare or valuable stock, such as a marine tank or a Koi pond which hold many thousands of pounds worth of livestock.

BIRDS

Birds have been kept in captivity by humans for centuries. One of the reasons for this is the diverse nature of birds. They have been kept for companionship, for hunting, and for eggs and meat. Beauty and practicality are words that describe some of the qualities humans value among birds.

History of birds

There are no clear records of who were the first to keep birds, but there are certainly records of Egyptian bird-keeping that go back as far as at least 4000BC. The Greeks are recorded as being the first people to keep parrots and parakeets, and they even used to employ slaves just to care for the parrots and to teach them to talk.

The Romans were also great bird lovers and are known to have had extensive aviaries, keeping most types of bird; talking birds were highly prized, as well as songbirds. Throughout the known world, parrots were kept as tame pets and, as is possible with the highly intelligent parrots, they tended to be house (or hut) pets that were allowed to roam free and live along side their people. Parrots were highly prized and their colourful feathers used in head-dresses and ceremonial customs.

The history of bird-keeping in Europe continued after the Romans although it was not well documented. More is known from the late 1400s onwards, with Christopher Columbus returning with Cuban Amazon parrots.

From the 1500s, canaries were very popular throughout Europe and were being bred by the farmers on the Canary Islands for export. This move towards captive breeding started the development of the different types of canary that we know today, including the traditional yellow canary.

The Victorians loved birds and built many public aviaries, as well as having caged birds in their homes. It was the Victorians that developed a passion for budgerigars, which were imported into this country by naturalist John Gould around 1840. By the end of that

BIRDS

century, large numbers of budgies had been imported and many people had started to breed these lovely little birds, thus producing the first of many colour 'sports'. In the process, the budgie became a popular pet and exhibition bird.

Bird-keeping today has moved on a long way from those first pet birds. Many species are available as pets, ranging from the largest of parrots to the smallest of finches. Most pet birds are captive-bred, with only a few of the rarer finches that are very difficult to breed needing to be imported.

In the UK, it is to be expected that the birds you buy will be captive-bred, but be aware of the more expensive parrots being offered for sale cheaply, the chances are they will have been wild-caught. This is unnecessary and causes parrots great trauma. Finches and some of the other smaller birds are not greatly affected by being caught as long as they are treated correctly and end up with responsible owners. With all the information and specialist equipment and foods available to modern pet owners, there is no excuse for not being responsible.

Acquiring a bird

Most people get their first bird from the local pet shop, and this an ideal start to bird-keeping. It is a good idea to do as much research as you can before you embark on a hobby that can become a huge part of your life.

When choosing a pet bird you need to look at what it is you want from a bird. If you want a pet to take for a walk, then bird keeping is not for you. If you want a pet that will cuddle down on the sofa, then bird-keeping is not for you – although some birds can be just as affectionate in their own way.

Having made sure you want a bird, the type of bird is the next consideration. Ask yourself the following questions:

- How much time will I have for my new pet?
- What space do I have in my home or garden for birds?
- Can I cope with any mess inside my house?

BIRDS

- What other pets and people have I got in my home and will bringing a bird into the house be fair on everyone including the new bird?
- What length of commitment am I prepared to give?
- How much money do I want to spend?

Time

If you have a lot of time (ideally you or a member of your family will be at home all day), then parrot species can make wonderful pets. They like company and you will get the most out of them if you can dedicate a lot of time to them. Parrots in the wild tend to live in huge flocks and so need a lot of social interaction in captivity.

If you have a lot of time then parrot species can make wonderful pets

You will also need a lot of time if you wish to breed your chosen birds, but depending on the species this does not mean you have to be there all day, as many birds want peace and quiet before breeding.

If you do not have much time, consider an aviary indoors or out, or a large cage of finches, canaries and other smaller birds, which will be happy to do their own thing all day if their basic requirements are met.

Space

Space is an important consideration, a large macaw will take up a lot of space, but a Senegal parrot will not

Space is an important consideration, a large macaw will take up a lot of space, but a Senegal parrot only requires a small amount of space in comparison. It will always be better to provide the largest living enclosure you can for your birds. For smaller birds, there are many nice indoor aviaries available that fit into modern homes while providing enough space for the birds. And, if you have the garden space, you can let your imagination run riot with the size and type of housing you provide for your birds. One word of caution though, if you are going to have an outdoor aviary, do think about the noise that your birds will make and whether your neighbours are going to appreciate it.

BIRDS

Mess

Birds can be very messy indoors. With a small bird like a budgie or canary, the main mess will be the seeds that get thrown from the cage, and feathers and dander when the bird moults. Feathers and dander can bring out allergies in some people. If you think you or a member of your household may be allergic to birds, you should visit a bird-keeper to see if you have a bad reaction, before bringing a new pet into your house.

Soft bill birds need moist food and fruit, and some species also require live food in the form of insects. All this can be extremely messy and so it is best that these birds are kept outside or in a room of their own.

If you have cats, think about where you house your bird or if it will be practical to keep birds with your cats

Other pets

If you have cats, think about where you house your bird or if it will be practical to keep birds with your cats. Many households are successful at getting the two species to live together, but many cats will hunt wild birds and may think your budgie in the cage is good to torment. Careful thought about where to keep the cage and the type of bird should resolve any problems before they occur.

Dogs and birds also need careful introductions and, again, it is wise to be cautious and not trust dogs and birds together. Having said that, some birds will turn the table and terrorise your dogs or cats! Make sure that when introducing new animals into your home you are not taking time away from those already there. It is especially important, if you are looking at getting a parrot as a pet, that all members of your household are happy with this. Parrots are extremely noisy and, although you may love the sound of your parrots competing with the TV, it may cause problems with your family, especially if not everyone feels the same about the parrots!

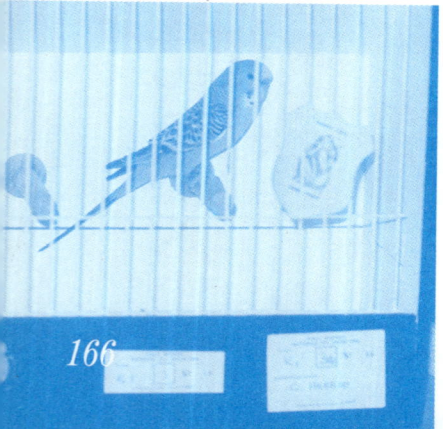

Show budgerigar in a show cage

BIRDS

Commitment

Not only will the day-to-day care of your birds take time, with many birds there is a long-term commitment to think about. Parrots live a long time, so, if you are not sure you want to share your life wiht one for the next 40 years, parrots are not going to be for you. Budgies or parakeets may be better, although you could still be looking at a pet that will live 20 years or more.

You must also think about who will look after your birds if you are ill or go on holiday. A bird in a cage can be moved to someone else's house for a short while, if absolutely necessary, but aviaries cannot. Would you be able to find someone to visit them or could you afford a house-sitter? Remember with small birds this may only be a relative short-term consideration, but parrots could outlive you. If you are going to share your life with one of these wonderful birds, your dedication to them must also include providing for them should the worst happen.

Money

You are only limited by your own budget. You could spend a fairly small amount on a small finch and its cage or you could spend thousands on a large parrot. Whatever bird you decide to bring into your home, remember that the cost is not just buying the bird, the cage and some food now and again, but veterinary care if needed can be very expensive for birds. For longer living species you may need to replace cages and equipment. Parrots can be very destructive and you may have to think about the cost of having to replace furniture and fittings within your house over time as well.

Choosing a bird

Although your local pet shop is the best place to start looking for your bird, most only keep in stock the basic budgies, canaries, a few finches, cockatiels and maybe a few other species of parakeet. If you want to start showing birds, then it

ACCESSORIES CHECK LIST

- Cage or aviary suitable for your type of bird
- Food bowls for seed, grit, soft foods/fruit
- Drinkers for water
- Food
- Cuttlefish bone
- Iodine block
- Perches of different sizes suitable for your bird
- Floor covering
- Cleaning-out tools
- Cover for the cage
- Toys for parrots and budgies
- Phone number of a good avian vet to hand

BIRDS

would be wise to search out your local bird club. They will be able to give you information on local shows and local breeders. Be aware though that a lot of breeders will only sell their stock at certain times of the year, so you may have to wait to get the bird you want.

If you want any other species, you may want to visit a bird specialist, who will know more about the type of birds you are looking for. If you are looking for a parrot of any sort, it is strongly recommended you find a reputable breeder. They will have the parents and the rest of the clutch and will also be able to provide you with all the details of your parrot from its hatching. You will have to go through the 'baby and teenage years' with your newly-born parrot, which with some of the larger birds can be as testing as with human children.

If you want to take on an older parrot, you can often find birds advertised for sale privately. Make sure you find out the real reason why the bird is being sold, in case it has a habit of screaming all night or biting any men it sees.

Rescue centres often have birds and if you want to take on anything other than a budgie or canary, you may want to search out a rescue centre that specialises in the type of bird you want.

One place never to buy a bird from is a bird auction. The birds will be stressed, could have travelled a long way and are often always old birds.

Good health

With all birds it is important to be aware of any signs of ill health. It is not worth buying a sick bird, even if it is cheap. It will only cost you dearly in vet's fees and emotionally when your pet of only a few days dies.

You should look out for signs of general activity. Any bird that is sitting still with its feathers puffed up, eyes closed and generally appearing sick is to be avoided. If the bird of your choice is active and generally looks all right, give it a closer inspection.

BIRDS

If it is in a large cage with other birds, don't be afraid to ask to have it caught and put into a smaller inspection cage.

Breathing should be even with no signs of wheezing. You should not be able to see the tail of a bird moving when it is breathing normally. This is an indication of laboured breath. Things that can cause laboured breathing include mites, fungal infections and parasites.

The bill of a bird should be clean and free from mites and deformities. Although overgrown bills can be trimmed and prevented from becoming worse again, it's an expensive job which should be left to an experienced bird-keeper or vet.

Mites can be treated, but this will be expensive and, if they have been left for too long without treatment, they can cause scarring on the bill of some larger birds. The mites are usually scaly face mites and can also be found on the legs of birds. Be warned though, if one bird has it, they will all have it as it spreads very quickly. If you take on a bird with mites and have others at home, you should quarantine your new bird for six weeks or more.

The bill of a bird should be clean and free from mites and deformities as with the mynah bird above

Feathers should look good and not too tatty, otherwise they are not too much of a health concern, but can be a good indication of how clean they have been kept. The main species whose plumage you need to take care with are parrots, budgies and other related birds. They are all susceptible to Psittacine Beak and Feather Disease (PBFD), a fatal disease that can cause a great deal of suffering to the bird. The feathers will look twisted and the bird will have bald patches.

Budgies can have a virus known as French moult. This, as the name suggests, causes feather loss. Always hold open the wings of a young bird as feather loss appears first in the flight and tail feathers. Feather loss can also be caused by feather plucking, usually starting through stress and, in most species, removing the cause of the stress will stop the problem. With parrots though, the bird may be so badly traumatised that it may take many years of careful treatment to solve the problem.

BIRDS

The legs and feet of any bird should be clean and free of mites and injury. Some of the finches tend to have very long, fast-growing claws, which will need clipping frequently. If the bird you have chosen has a ring on its leg, make sure it is free turning. The rings are used for identification purposes and, with parrots, should be kept on where possible in case your bird escapes. On smaller pet birds it should be removed, as they can get seeds stuck down them, which can cause injury. If you leave the ring on then do check them regularly. In most cases rings are not an indication of age, unless they are closed rings, with the year stamped on them. One of the only ways you have of aging most birds is to look at the legs and feet for scaling that appears as they get older.

For signs of weight loss, always check the breastbone of any bird. Although in some species you will not find as much muscle as in others, the chest should feel plump and firm, and the breastbone should not protrude too much. Avoid birds that show signs of weight loss as this can be an indication of disease.

Feeding

There are so many types of birds and they all have different requirements for food. The one thing the different types have in common is that they must always have fresh water available at all times. You will need to change your bird's water at least daily and with some birds two or three times a day. Some birds are messier than others, but they all get food in the water! There are many types of water dispensers available from your local pet shop; some birds will drink from a water bottle, which will keep the water fresh, but most won't and you will need to use a drinker that they can get their whole beak into. With most of the smaller birds, as long as the water is up off the floor, you will tend to get just seed husks in it, but with bigger birds like softbills and parrots, they will dunk their food into the water. This is natural behaviour, but makes more work for you!

All food should be placed in a clean food container. There is a wide choice available and your choice will be dependent on the type of bird you are feeding. Make sure bowls are clean at all

It is worth considering acquiring birds in pairs as they can get lonely

BIRDS

times. It can be a good idea to have a spare set of food bowls and use them in rotation.

Birds are either seedeaters or softbills and the diet they require will depend on which group they fall into. Softbills include birds such as zosterops, bulbuls, mynah birds, glossy starlings, pekin robins and one of the largest softbills, the toucan. Seedeaters include budgies, parakeets, finches, canaries, parrots and most other pet birds you can think of.

The softbill's diet has improved greatly over the past few years as more and more commercial food has become available, making it easier for the owner to provide a complete diet. The main part of the softbill's food is made up of insects and fruit. The basic commercial mix, which will need to be fed dampened (carrot or fruit juice is very good for this), will need changing at least twice a day and more often in hot weather. You can get live food for your birds from most good pet shops and in larger quantities via mail order. The most common live foods found are mealworms, crickets, locusts, fruit flies and maggots (although it is better to raise these yourself). White worms and microworm cultures can be bought for you to raise. These are ideal for the very small birds, especially when feeding young. Some of the larger softbills like the toucans would also eat small mammals in the wild and small frozen mice are available in the reptile section of most pet shops.

Fruit is also a very good addition to the diet, but again make sure it remains fresh and be prepared to change it during the day in hot weather. Berries such as blackberries are enjoyed by most birds and can be collected and frozen when in season for use throughout the year. If no fresh fruit is available, you can use tinned fruit in natural juice, but this should only be a standby. Dried fruit can be fed dried or soaked before feeding according to your birds' preferences.

Birds are either seedeaters or softbills and the diet they require will depend on which group they fall into

Seedeaters have a wider choice of foods readily available to them, with many commercial seed mixes pre-packed in the shops. If you just have one pet bird such as a budgie or canary,

BIRDS

you will find feeding very cheap, so always go for the best you can. It is better to buy a smaller amount of food so it will remain fresh. Pre-packed food will be fresher than loose seed and free from contaminants such as dust, dirt and water.

The basic diet for most seedeaters is a mix of different types of seed in varying quantities; these have been developed over the years to provide the best nutrition for each type of bird. It is important to feed the right sort of mix to each bird. Canary mix, for example, has a high proportion of oil-based seeds, which have a higher fat content; this mix will also have seeds higher in protein content. Budgie mix, however, contains more cereal seeds that have higher carbohydrate levels, and less fat and protein content. You will find that there are several types of budgie mix as they have different requirements at different times, ie maintenance mix, breeding mix and moulting mix.

The range of foods for parakeets and parrots has increased over the past few years. At one time the available diets for these birds was very poor, but now you can get good quality mixes for small and large parrots, different mixes for Amazon parrots and African species, as well as for the larger macaws.

All seedeaters require additional fresh foods and these can range from chickweed and other green foods, which can either be collected from the wild (please make sure no pesticides have been used and collect any wild greens away from roads) or from the supermarket. Fresh fruit is enjoyed by all birds. In particular, certain species of parrots need a range of fruit within their diet.

You can also feed all birds egg food. It is made, as the name suggests, from a high concentration of eggs and will cause your bird to put on weight if fed all the time. It can be fed dry or moist, although you need to check it regularly in hot weather. Egg food is best kept as a pick-me-up food to be given if your bird is unwell or during the moult and breeding season. It was first developed to help birds feed their young.

An important thing to watch out for with seedeaters is how much seed they have left. Because the husks of the seeds often fall back into the food bowl it can look as though the food bowl

BIRDS

is full when in fact it is just full of husks. Some birds also dislike having to pick through the husks to find seed. To prevent your bird starving – and birds have reportedly starved to death this way – blow gently over the top of the seeds in the food bowl to remove the husks.

You can get many different types of food supplement for birds, some are sprinkled on the food, some are water-soluble. Although any bird that eats a varied diet should not need any supplements, very few birds eat all or enough of what they should. Birds can be as fussy as us and pick out the nicest bits first! So it is a good idea to give some sort of supplement two or three times a week.

The other thing that is important to remember for seedeaters is to provide grit. This comes in two main forms, mineral grit and oyster shell grit; pick a size appropriate to your bird's size. The purpose of grit is to help the gizzard grind up the seed ready for digestion, thus replacing the job that teeth do in other animals.

Cuttlefish bone will help to provide calcium and birds enjoy picking at it; you can buy cleaned cuttlefish bone at all good pet shops. You may also find it lying on the beach and, if you have the time and patience to prepare it, this can be used for your birds. It will need soaking and boiling several times and then drying out thoroughly before it's ready. Iodine blocks placed in the cage and charcoal both have a beneficial effect on the digestive system.

Once you have chosen which type of bird you are going to keep, then you need to get their housing ready

Caging

Once you have chosen which type of bird you are going to keep, then you need to get their housing ready. It is advisable to do this before you bring your bird home. For any bird that is to be housed in the home, please provide the largest cage you have space for.

Indoor aviaries are very popular these days and are relatively cheap compared to other cages. They often come on wheels so

BIRDS

you can move your birds around for easy cleaning. Alternatively you could build a more permanent aviary in your home. Many bird-keepers use a spare room as a bird room and fit it out with aviaries and breeding cages: choose a room that has stable heating and lighting.

Make sure you choose a cage that will be easy for you to clean and that has the right bar spacing for the type of bird you have chosen. Avoid very fancy cage shapes as these are made to please you and not the birds, and the space is quite often wasted. Choose the best shape for your birds, eg parrots like climbing space, so a cage with length and height are good for them, but canaries and finches don't use the bars to climb at all, so cages that are longer will suit them better.

Parrots need very strong bars, they have beaks designed for cracking nuts, so bars have to be strong enough to cope with them and have good catches on the doors: it doesn't take long for inquisitive parrots to try and open their cage door. Some parrot owners use special parrot stands for their birds and, although these are very good for giving your bird exercise during the day, you must still provide a cage as a place for the bird to feel secure. Regardless of the size of bird they must be able to open their wings out full-stretch in every direction. Many pet birds can be given exercise outside the cage and for parrots this helps with the space issue. Because they are such large birds, providing very large cages in the home can be difficult.

The placing of your bird's cage at home is very important. Kitchens are totally impractical, not only would it be unhygienic, with unstable temperatures, but non-stick pans can give off fumes that are poisonous to birds.

Living rooms are good, allowing your bird to interact with you more, but you must still take care about the placing of the cage. Avoid windows where strong sunlight might make your bird too hot; avoid draughty doorways and site your cage away from electrical equipment such as televisions and noisy hi-fi systems.

It can help your bird to be more settled if you have a cover for the cage at night. This must be of a material thick enough to

Parrots need very strong bars, as they have beaks designed for cracking nuts

BIRDS

block out the light, but still allow a good air flow through the cage. Only use this to help create a longer night-time for your bird while you are using your living room at night.

As for outdoor aviaries, these are only limited by the amount of space and money you have. If you have a very small garden in close proximity to neighbours, parrots and parakeets (apart from the smallest species) will not be a good idea. Your neighbours really will not want to be woken at dawn by loud squawking! The noise can be controlled by the use of attached indoor accommodation to house the birds overnight, but they will still be noisy during the day.

Try and avoid building your aviary in view of roads as not only will this disturb your birds, but it could be tempting for thieves. You may want to provide heat and light in your aviary (light is especially important if you need to tend to your birds in the evening), so being near an electric source will be important.

There are many different designs of aviary but the basic design consists of a flight area and overnight accommodation for the birds, normally in the form of an adapted shed. The other very important item is a safety porch to allow you easy access without the birds escaping. This can lead into the shelter or into the aviary itself, but it is important that it will not disturb the birds as you come and go.

Make sure you have plenty of perches as well as a flight area. Perches need to be of varying sizes to exercise the birds' feet and this applies in cages as well. Types of perches range from wooden dowelling rods, branches from fruit trees (make sure they have not been sprayed with pesticides) and commercially available perches made of plastic or wood. You can buy perches that will help keep your birds' claws worn down, as well as swings and carousels.

In an aviary you have the space to provide your birds with a more natural habitat. You can either plant the aviary with suitable plants or, if you have chosen a solid base that is easier to clean and will help stop vermin, use plants in pots.

You will need to do a lot of planning before building an aviary, far more than can be covered in this book. Be sure to research

BIRDS

your chosen birds' requirements, as different species will have different requirements for their housing.

Daily care

All birds need your attention daily. How much will depend on the type of birds you have chosen. Smaller seedeaters such as canaries and finches will just need a few moments of your time morning and evening.

While you are feeding and changing water, make sure you observe your birds' behaviour, any changes may be the first signs of illness and the earlier you can spot something going wrong the easier it will be to treat.

If breeding, your birds have to fancy each other – they will not co-operate with the 'wrong' partner

Birds in an outdoor aviary will have the benefit of rain to keep their feathers clean, but indoor birds will need your help. Most birds will require spraying with water about twice a week. Some will enjoy a bath placed in the cage and will relish a good splash around. If your bird will not use a birdbath, you will have to spray it; this can be done with a clean plant sprayer. Use tepid water and gently spray upwards towards your bird from a distance so they are lightly covered with water. It may take a few times before they really enjoy it, but when they do many will hold open their wings for an all-over shower! Giving your bird a bath or shower will make everything in the cage wet, so it is a good idea to remove food first, to keep it dry. It will also make an ideal time for a cage clean.

Cleaning

Cages and aviary bird rooms should be cleaned twice a week; some messy birds may need more than this. Flight areas can be cleaned less often. All birds create a mess of dust and food. If you have a lot of birds in a bird room, you may want to wear a mask to protect yourself from the dust while cleaning.

There are many different floor coverings that can be used in cages, from old newspapers, sand sheets, loose sand, wood

BIRDS

chips (of the pet bedding type, not the sort used in gardens), newspaper based pet bedding and many more. Choose one that will be safe for your bird. If you have a parrot or parakeet that is likely to chew up anything in the cage, it must be safe if ingested, so newspapers and wood chip may be the best bet. Finches and canaries will be happy with most floor coverings, but some coverings will make more mess outside the cage than others.

In an aviary, the floor of the bird room should be easy to clean, with the main area of mess underneath food containers and perches. The flights will not need quite so much cleaning.

Check that the food and water is clean and fresh on a daily basis, and that the cage is in good repair and safe. Check your bird's appearance – look for any signs of illness or unusual behaviour. The feet and beak should be clean, with bright alert eyes. If you are worried about your bird do consult a good avian vet as soon as possible.

In an aviary, make sure you have plenty of perches as well as a flight area – perches should vary in size

Breeding

Breeding birds is not as simple as with many other types of pets. There are so many types of birds and they all have different requirements to persuade them to breed. Some are all too willing and will have a go in the smallest of cages, while others may take years of preparation and persuasion. Others still will happily breed, but fail when it comes to hatching or rearing the babies. And of course your birds have to fancy each other in the first place; many will just not co-operate with the 'wrong' partner.

If you are really interested in breeding birds, the best place to start would be at your local bird club. You will find local clubs all over the country as well as national species clubs. You will find there are many happy to help new bird-keepers and this can be an excellent way of obtaining good breeding stock.

Showing

The same rule for breeding applies to showing birds. Local clubs will hold their own shows several times a year and you

BIRDS

will be able to assess the quality of your birds and get help with the preparation that needs to take place before a show. You will also need special show cages; different ones for different species of birds.

There is a long history of showing birds in the UK and although there is some modern day objection to it from animal rights activists, it is a very important part of bird keeping as it is how new skills are passed on and, without the skills to breed birds, many species today would have become extinct. Indeed, there are many more species that may need help in the future.

Different species

Budgerigars

Budgerigars are the birds most people think of as a pet and the starting point for many bird-keepers. They are small, with a length of about 7cm, can be easily trained, are interactive with their owners and can be very cheap to keep. These make them one of the world's most popular pets.

They originate from Australia and can still be found in huge flocks in the outback. They are smaller members of the parrot family and share much of the behaviour of big parrots, just in miniature.

The wild colour of a budgie is a light green with a yellow face and forehead; they have six black spots on the throat with small, violet-blue cheek patches. The back of the head and the wings are barred with black and the tail is a greenish-blue underneath.

They have been bred in large numbers since the 19th century and this has led to the development of many colour varieties.

They are easy to sex: the male has a blue cere (the fleshy bump above the beak) and the female a brown cere. The colour intensifies as the bird matures and comes into breeding condition. Babies are easy to recognise as the barring on the head reaches down to the cere, gradually moving back as the bird moults to its adult plumage. They have black eyes without the white ring, while birds that are just out of the nest have

Budgerigars are the birds most people think of as a pet and the starting point for many bird keepers

BIRDS

black marks on their beaks, although these are absent in yellow or white birds.

The only disadvantage to buying a very young bird is that it can be more difficult to sex, although this should not be that important in pet birds.

If you want a pet that will become hand-tame and talkative, then it is best to get your budgie as young as possible. The fact that it is easy to recognise a young bird helps, although they are only available during the breeding season, so do be prepared to wait for that special bird.

Feeding budgies is very easy. There are lots of commercial budgie mixes and they will also enjoy millet sprays and green foods. Budgies also need an iodine block to help their thyroid work correctly. A favoured food of budgies is chickweed, which can be collected from the wild, but make sure that the area where you collect the chickweed is free from pesticides, chemical sprays or car fumes.

Budgies will happily live outside in aviaries, although they will need shelter and some heating if it is very cold. They will live happily with other birds, including cockatiels and some of the larger finches, but are happiest in large groups of their own kind. Indoors they make fantastic pets for young and old, proving to be very easy to care for. It is because they naturally occur in very large flocks that they are so sociable towards human beings and although it is lovely to have a tame and talking bird, unless you are able to be with it most of the time, they can get quite lonely.

It is worth considering having two budgies, as it is possible to have two talking birds together. Get one bird first and add another, once the first bird is tame and talking. It can happen that the first bird will teach the new bird to talk. Single birds that get lonely can sometimes have behavioural problems, which can cause stress to both bird and owner, spoiling the enjoyment of the relationship.

The average lifespan for budgies is about seven years, but birds kept and bred in aviaries may not live this long. Pampered pet budgies may live for 10 or more years. Budgies do like to play,

BIRDS

so make sure you have lots of toys in the cage. You can find a huge number of toys to keep budgies happy, everything from ladders, unbreakable mirrors, balls, bells and plastic budgies (for company!) to toys that dispense food if this or that part is pulled. Budgies are clever birds and great fun can be had thinking up games for them.

Colour varieties in budgies number in the many hundreds, having been developed by fanciers all over the world. There are different colours, shades and markings, all of which have numerous combinations. When looking for your perfect birds remember that not all types will be available at any one time nor can any breeder have many different types, most will specialise in one or two colours.

Some colours found in budgies are green, blue, yellow, white, violet and grey. And if you take the colour green, you can have light green, medium green and dark green; in blues you can have sky blue, cobalt and mauve; in yellows you will find light yellow, medium yellow and olive yellow; and many more shades in-between. Then you can have either white or yellow on the faces – the first blue budgies to be bred only had white faces, but you can now get yellow-faced blues.

Colours can be combined, so you can have yellow and green, and blue and white. These birds are called pieds. There are two forms of pieds: dominant and recessive. The recessive tend to be a bit smaller, a bit more nervous and the iris of the eye in a recessive is a deep plum colour, while the dominant has the normal coloured budgie eyes.

The black markings on the wings have their own set of varieties: cinnamon dilutes the colour (and also gives the bird reddish eyes) and opalines change the markings, giving the bird a V-shaped area free of marking at the top of the wings. The black markings can also be replaced by colour so you can have white wings, yellow wings and other colours. In spangles, the centres of the dark markings have a paler area and are very pretty.

Feather mutations also occur, with the crested forms being the most popular. The tufted has a tuft at the front of its head and the crested has a circular crest on the top of its head. These can be combined with any colour.

Not all of the genes that make up budgie varieties can be combined, but breeders over the years have tried most combinations. More are being developed all the time, so hunt out the specialist budgie clubs for recent developments.

Showing budgies is taken very seriously and many people invest a lot of time and effort into producing the best bird possible. Show birds are much bigger, but breeders who are looking for show stock wait until the birds have gone through one or two moults before letting them go to new homes, so they can see over time which birds are best to keep.

You should ensure that the floor of the bird room in an aviary is easy to clean

Cockatiels

Cockatiels are another member of Australia's large parrot family, they are sociable birds that live in flocks in the wild. They share many features of the cockatoo ('cockatiel' is the Portuguese for 'little cockatoo'). Both cockatiels and cockatoos have a crest that they can raise up and down to express themselves. The other feature they share is that both cocks and hens sit during the incubation of the eggs, whereas in other parrots only the hen sits.

The cockatiel is classed as a parakeet along with budgies and other small parrot species. They are about 30cm long and, although louder than budgies, are not as noisy as a larger bird would be.

Colour varieties in budgies number in the many hundreds, having been developed by fanciers all over the world

Cockatiels were brought to Europe at about the same time as budgies, but, being a little bit bigger, they have never been quite as popular as the budgie. They can be taught to talk and are very good at learning to whistle simple tunes. Both sexes can do this equally well, so although sexing them as young birds is very difficult it will not make too much difference for pet birds.

The natural colour of the cockatiel is grey, with the cock birds having a yellow face, round red patches on each cheek and white

BIRDS

Cockatiels, part of Australia's large parrot family, share many features of the cockatoo

feathers on the edges of the wings. The hen bird is very similar, but the head has a grey frosting over the yellow feathers and the underside of the hen's tail is barred. Young birds look very similar to the hens, the cock birds developing their brighter colours as they get older.

There are not as many varieties of cockatiels as there are budgies. Typical types are listed below.

- Cinnamons are a warm brown shade, with all other markings the same as normal.
- Pearl is a mark variety giving a lacy look to the feather markings. The cock birds lose this effect as they get older.
- Lutinos are white birds retaining the yellow and red parts of the plumage.
- Pieds have yellow markings all over the body.
- Fallow is similar to the cinnamon, but with a yellow tinge to it and red eyes.
- Silver is a very pretty delicate silver grey and the rest of the markings as normal.
- Whiteface cockatiels have pure white faces instead of the yellow and red.

Any of these can be combined together, although some are sex-linked or recessive varieties that will affect the look of the combination and the ability to combine. Cockatiel genetics is a very interesting subject and far too complicated for this book to cover.

Feeding cockatiels is very easy. Follow the same guidelines as for budgies, although buy a designated cockatiel mix rather than one for budgies. The main difference in the mixes is the inclusion of sunflower seeds. They will play with toys and can be very amusing to watch.

Cockatiels will breed very readily, including in cages, but will always produce the best results in outdoor aviaries. They will

Cockatoos are not as widely kept as other parrots, but they do make fantastic pets

BIRDS

also breed all year round, so it is a good idea to restrict the breeding only to the warmer months to give your birds a rest. They will breed from about a year old and will continue throughout their life. Cockatiels can live well into their twenties, but young birds should be saved for breeding while older birds are retired.

You can often find hand-reared cockatiels for sale. These have usually been reared in a cage by the breeder from four or five weeks onwards, so they are almost at fledging, but finishing them off with total human contact makes for very tame, steady birds who will accept their new homes without too much stress. And, of course, all the hard work of getting them hand-tame has already been done. You will need to keep the contact up or your bird will soon lose interest in you and become naughty, as all parrots species can!

Other parakeets

Some of the nicest birds to keep in an aviary are the small parakeets. Some of them can be kept indoors and become tame, but most of them are happier in aviaries with room to fly and the company of their own kind. As they share the curiosity of all parrot species, they can be tamed and, if you spend time letting them get to know you, they will soon start investigating you. Most of them are very quiet, making them ideal for urban gardens and, being small, they are not very destructive. They will feed on the same diet as cockatiels and have very similar housing requirements.

Some commonly found parakeet species are described below.

- Bourke's parakeets are a very pretty pink, with blue feathers on the outer edge of the wings. The hens lack most of the blue colouring. They are very small, at only 21cm long. They come from Australia, are fairly crepuscular and live in groups of about 10 birds. They breed easily and raise clutches of about four or five chicks, although seven is not unusual. They are very quiet birds, so are ideal for urban gardens. They will live in a mixed aviary.

BIRDS

- Splendid grass parakeets, again, are only 21cm, but they are extremely colourful. The head and neck is sea blue, the back is green and the chest area is yellow, with the cock birds having red feathers on the crop and extending down to the chest. The tail is green with yellow and black feathers and the wings are a greenish blue, with bright blue and black at the edge. The female is darker on the back than the male and has an olive green breast area. She has less blue than the male. A quiet friendly little bird that will add colour to an aviary.

- Turquoisine parakeets also only get to 21cm. They are quiet and, if not breeding, will live with other birds, but will be aggressive while breeding. They can live outside during the winter as long as they have been bred outside, otherwise it is best to give them extra heat. The cock birds have a sky blue head, yellow to green undersides, green neck, throat and back, and have red and blue on the wings and flight feathers. The female does not have red on the wings and has less blue in general.

- Other species you will see offered for sale are red rumped parakeet, blue wing parakeet as well as many more.

Most of the parakeet species are from Australia; some others are from further afield. Species available include: Barraband's parakeet, Princess of Wales parakeet, ringneck parakeet and the Alexandrine parakeet.

The larger species of parakeets that are available need roughly the same conditions as the smaller birds, but with proportionately more space.

Lovebirds

Peach-faced lovebirds come from Africa and have been bred in captivity for many years now. There are many colour varieties of the lovebird including pastels, yellows, pieds and blues. The normal colouring is a dark green with bright blue over the rump; the face is, as the name suggests, a bright peach colour. When young they have dark markings on their beaks. There is no way of telling the difference between the sexes.

BIDS

Lovebirds are kept more often as aviary birds or for breeding than as pets, although they should be given a higher ranking as pets. This is probably because they are always sold in pairs and require a partner to bond with. This can be a human, if they have enough time to devote to their bird. Look out for hand-reared birds, these will be steady and accustomed to people.

Lovebirds really do have wonderful little characters, although this does not always show when kept in pairs. They may get on with other birds in the aviary, but they can become aggressive towards other birds at any time.

Feeding is the same as for all parrot-like birds of this size, although you can get a specialised lovebird mix.

There are other species of lovebird not so widely seen such as the fisher's lovebird and the masked lovebird.

Rosellas

If you have more space you may like to look at keeping some of the larger parakeets and rosellas. Rosellas come from Australia and the most commonly available is the golden mantle rosella. This bird is highly colourful with a bright red head, yellow body, black and yellow on the back and blue on the wings. Golden mantles are about 30cm long. They breed easily in the aviary, but are not good house pets. They live for up to 15 years or so and will breed for most of that time. They live in a flock in the wild and spend a lot of time on the ground. All rosellas should be given a good parakeet mix.

Other species include crimson rosella, western rosella, and Brown's rosella.

Conures

Conures are parakeets from central and South America. They make really good birds for aviaries and breeding, and many species are available. Many of them make excellent pets.

Parrots

Parrots are wonderful pets to keep and challenging birds to breed. They come in many different sizes and colours. Parrots

Peach-faced lovebirds come from Africa and have been bred in captivity for many years

BIRDS

are often misunderstood and deprived of the chance to display their natural behaviour. They have been kept in captivity for thousands of years, highly prized for their ability to mimic the human voice and other sounds around them.

You don't have to have a huge amount of space to keep parrots; you just need to choose the right size for your home. Some of the smaller species are only 12cm in length and will live quite happily in a cage and some will even breed in cages. The largest parrots can be up to 40cm in length, so these species need as much space as you can provide.

Some of the smaller species include the blue crowd hanging parrot. At 12cm this is one of the smallest parrots and, although it can be kept and bred in a large cage, its diet means it is too messy for most homes and is better kept in an aviary. Unlike other parrots it eats nectar with all sorts of additional foodstuffs, such as hard-boiled eggs, rice, fruit and ant eggs.

The Senegal and the Meyer parrot are two very similar, small parrots, both about 22cm in length. They come from Africa and make very good pets, as well as ideal aviary birds. You often see hand-reared Senegals for sale and these make especially good pets. They are fun, amusing and the perfect way to have a parrot without needing lots of space. They will breed in cages as well as in aviaries. You can now buy commercial food mixes specifically for these birds from most good pet shops.

The parrots that most people keep are the medium-sized birds such as the African greys and the Amazon parrots.

African greys are thought of as the best parrot for talking, although it is no guarantee that any individual will learn to talk. You need a lot of patience and time to teach any bird to talk. They are a nice size at 35cm and are highly social birds living in the wild in huge flocks. As the name suggests, the African grey has grey plumage, but it has a red tail. The irises of its eyes are yellow and the underside of the body is a lighter grey.

Feeding has become easier in the last few years with the introduction of specialist foods for them, but do make sure you give them plenty of fresh foods as well. Greys will get bored

Parrots are wonderful pets to keep and challenging birds to breed

BIRDS

very easily and need plenty of stimulation if they are not to become feather pluckers.

African greys will breed very easily, often in cages, but they are not the best parents, so the babies have to be hand reared, which isn't always a bad thing as hand-reared birds can make very tame pets.

Amazon parrots are predominantly green and, depending on the species, have varying amount of other colours running through their plumage. They come from central and South America, and are about 38cm in length. Again, specialist foods are available for Amazons and fresh foods are a must. You cannot sex them visually, although it is relatively easy to get birds DNA-sexed these days – ask your vet for advice.

Generally, Amazons are very good at talking and will mimic household sounds as well as whistling. They do unfortunately have a very loud and piercing screech, so to have an Amazon in your home you need to really want them there.

The orange winged Amazon is the most common species; you will also see the mealy Amazon, white fronted Amazon, blue fronted Amazon and many others.

Cockatoos
Cockatoos are not as widely kept as other parrots, even though they make fantastic pets. They have excellent talking ability and are very intelligent birds. Most cockatoos are white with some yellow round their head crest, which they can raise at will to express their emotions, although some species are pink, grey or black.

Cockatoos are some of the most long-lived parrots, many reaching up to 100 years of age. They become very attached to their owners, however, often to the point of excluding other members of the family from their affections.

Some of the species you will see available are the greater and lesser sulphur crested cockatoo, the umbrella cockatoo, roseate cockatoo, Goffin's cockatoo and the Galah cockatoo.

Undertake plenty of research into these birds and their needs to make sure they are for you before you purchase one. If you decide that you can offer a cockatoo all that it needs, then you will have a bird that will become a member of your family for years to come.

Macaws

When people think of a pirate's parrot this is what will usually come to mind, the blue and gold macaw. These are big, majestic parrots that need lots of space and time, but which will reward you with great affection. However, be prepared to have your house destroyed, as they have very powerful beaks and can be very destructive. They are also extremely noisy.

For those not lucky enough to have a lot of space at home but who would still like to have the fun of owning a macaw, there is the Hahn's macaw. At only 33cm, they are ideal. They are not as long-lived as the larger macaws – their lifespan only averaging about 20 years – but they have all the personality and requirements of the larger birds.

The most stunning macaw is the hyacinth macaw, which at 100cm is the biggest of the species, with stunning deep purple-blue plumage. Unfortunately, they are very rare and extremely expensive, and because of their endangered species status all individuals should be part of specialist breeding programmes.

Macaws commonly available include the blue and gold, scarlet, green winged and military macaws.

Lories and lorikeets

Two other groups of parrots that are growing in popularity are the lories and lorikeet. These are unusual in that, instead of having a seed-based diet, they feed on nectar and pollen. They have a brush-like protrusion on the end of the tongue with which they scoop up the nectar from flowers. These days there are commercial mixes specially designed for them, thus making feeding them less of a problem than it once was. They will also require a lot of fruit in the diet depending on the species. The downside to this is that their droppings are rather loose and messy, but, if you allow for this when planning an indoor cage, it is perfectly possible to keep them as pets.

BIRDS

Lories and lorikeets are very colourful and extremely playful, and delightful to have as companions. They will also breed fairly readily in an outdoor aviary. Species to look out for are green napped lorikeet, red lory, and the chattering lory.

Canaries

Canaries are the most popular cage bird after the budgie, ideal for keeping in the home as well as in an aviary. They are cheerful little birds with a delightful song. Feeding canaries is very easy, with many commercial mixes available, and the addition of green food and egg food when breeding. They will breed readily in indoor cages, as well as in an aviary, where they will mix well with other birds, although two cock canaries may fight.

There are many different types of canary. The border canary is the most popular, first bred in a bright yellow, but now available in white, blue, and cinnamon with more being developed all the time.

Gloster canaries are lively little canaries that not only have charming characters but are also good songsters. They are often used to foster other birds' chicks, as they are such good parents. Glosters come in two types: coronas – these are crested birds – and consorts, which are non-crested. Coronas cannot be bred together because of a genetically lethal factor that prevents the babies surviving.

Red factors are, as the name suggests, red coloured canaries. A true red factor will have an orange tinge to the feathers. The red colour can be enhanced by the use of special colour food. But be warned: there are those who will feed it to normal canaries, then sell them as red factors for a higher price. When the next moult occurs you will have a yellow bird!

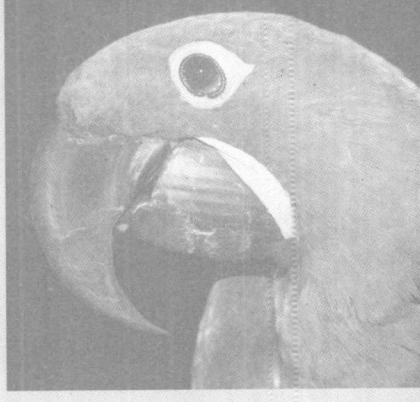

The hyacinth macaw is very rare and represents the pinnacle of parrot keeping

Canaries are the most popular cage bird after the budgie

BIRDS

The lizard canary looks very distinctive with its feathers looking as though they have reptiles' scales on them, hence the name. Lizards are another variety that, for the show bench, is colour fed, although this is not needed for good health.

Other types include the roller canary, bred for its singing ability; the Yorkshire canary, which is a tall thin bird; and the Fife canary, a small round bird similar to the border canary.

There are many different variations and feather types. Showing canaries is taken very seriously and there are many local and national clubs. If you want to breed or show your canary it is good to seek out the help of other local breeders.

Finches

Finches are a huge group of birds that are charming and small in size. Although they do not usually become tame, they will become used to their keepers. Most finches will do better in an aviary, while some will only breed in an aviary and may need others of their own kind to encourage breeding.

Finches can be split into two groups: Asian and Australasian finches. Asian finches on the whole are duller birds and are not that suitable to be kept in cages, apart from the Bengalese finch.

Some of the species of finches available are:

- Zebra finch – the most well-known and popular finch and deservedly so. Easy to breed in cages as well as aviaries, they are cheeky little birds with big personalities. They make ideal beginners' birds.

- Bengalese finch – the next most common finch, breeding easily in both cages and aviaries, although there is no way to sex these birds. If you wish to breed them, it is best to have a group of birds and let them pair up naturally.

- St Helena waxbill – a pretty finch, brown with a red flash over the eye. They will breed quite happily in an aviary if they are the only pair of their kind.

A finch in a show cage: There is a long history of showing birds in the UK

BIRDS

- Orange cheeked waxbills are only 10cm in size. These make a great addition to the aviary, although they will breed in cages.
- Cut throats – the cock bird has a bright red band around its throat, the hen lacks this band. Cut throats will breed in cages and aviaries, but are noisy and will inspect and destroy other birds' nests, so they should only be kept with birds of the same size or bigger.

There are hundreds of species of finch and, although the showing of these birds is not as popular as some of the other bird species, you will still find specialist clubs or local clubs with finch sections. Contacting other breeders will be the best way of getting pairs, as some finches can be very difficult to sex.

The macaw is a big majestic parrot that needs lots of space and time, rewarding you with great affection

Conclusion

If you decide that bird-keeping is for you, it can be tempting to try and keep lots of different species of bird, but it is best to start off slowly with one or two species and get used to keeping them, before laying out on expensive aviaries and equipment.

If you are looking for a pet bird, remember that a lot of species are long-lived, so be honest about how much time you want to give them and if you're likely to change your living arrangements.

But the most important thing is to enjoy your birds and they will reward you tenfold with their affection, beauty and charm.

Acknowledgements

Editor
Nick Mays

Authors
Marianne Brett - Cats and Dogs
Nick Mays - Small Mammals (except Ferrets)
Lucie Mann - Birds and Ferrets
David Green - Fish

Cover designer
Kurt Young

Text designer
Kurt Young

Editorial management: **Emma Hayley, Jenny Ross**

Photography
Marc Henrie

Photography - ardea.com: **John Daniels, Michel Labat, James Marchington, Johan De Meester, Brian Bevan, Ken Lucas, Liz Bomford, Andrey Zvoznikov, Rolf Kopfle**

Comstock.com, photos.com

Cover photography:
John Daniels/ardea.com, Ken Lucas /ardea.com, Johan De Meester/ardea.com, photos.com, Marc Henrie